THE DENIAL OF SCIENCE

THE DENIAL OF SCIENCE

Analysing climate change scepticism in the UK

Martin Lack

Author of the *Lack of Environment* blog

AuthorHouse™
1663 Liberty Drive
Bloomington, IN 47403
www.authorhouse.com
Phone: 1-800-839-8640

© 2013 by Martin Lack. All rights reserved.

No part of this book may be reproduced, stored in a retrieval system, or transmitted by any means without the written permission of the author.

Published by AuthorHouse   02/23/2013

ISBN: 978-1-4817-8397-2 (sc)
ISBN: 978-1-4817-8398-9 (e)

Any people depicted in stock imagery provided by Thinkstock are models, and such images are being used for illustrative purposes only.
Certain stock imagery © Thinkstock.

This book is printed on acid-free paper.

Because of the dynamic nature of the Internet, any web addresses or links contained in this book may have changed since publication and may no longer be valid. The views expressed in this work are solely those of the author and do not necessarily reflect the views of the publisher, and the publisher hereby disclaims any responsibility for them.

Contents

Preface vii
List of Abbreviations xi

Introduction 1
Background 9
Organisations 18
Scientists 25
Economists 30
Journalists 36
Politicians 43
Others 52
Discussion 57
Summary 65
Conclusions 75

Bibliography 77
Appendix—Supporting Evidence 95

"Earthrise"—Apollo 8, the first manned mission to the moon, entered lunar orbit on Christmas Eve, Dec. 24, 1968. Image Credit: NASA

Preface

"Once a photograph of the Earth taken from the outside is available – once the sheer isolation of the Earth becomes plain – a new idea as powerful as any in history will be let loose."
Sir Fred Hoyle FRS (1915-2001).

The above statement is all the more impressive when you consider that it was uttered by the world-famous astronomer in 1948. However, for many, it is a prophecy that came true twenty years later, when NASA astronomer William Anders took the iconic Apollo 8 'Earthrise' photo on 24 December 1968. In the years that followed, former World Bank economist Herman Daly would become famous for advocating what he called a steady-state economy. This he neatly summarised in his blunt assertion that, "the World may be developing but it is not growing!" Sadly, the fact that perpetual growth on a finite planet is impossible to sustain indefinitely seems as far from being accepted today as it was when Daly (and others) started highlighting it over 40 years ago.

The time is long overdue for us all to admit that the scales of many human activities now exceed the capacity of our environment to sustain them; or assimilate and recycle the wastes they generate. Using a passing river as a source of water, a laundry, and a toilet is OK if you live in a sparsely populated wilderness. However, when you live in an overcrowded slum it is likely to lead to your premature death. Given the sevenfold increase in the global human population—and an even greater increase in the number of animals reared by humans—a frontier mentality is no longer sustainable. It therefore seems very clear to me that all our environmental and pollution problems arise from our collective failure to acknowledge this reality. This has nothing whatsoever to do with being anti-human or anti-progress. It is simply a biological reality; and a facet of the global ecosystem of which we are a constituent part. This is a fact we forget or deny at our peril.

Many things that we humans do have therefore become a problem simply because of the scale at which we are now doing them. This includes pumping carbon dioxide into the atmosphere at such a rate that we will soon have doubled its concentration since the Industrial Revolution. OK, so I have declared an interest: I accept the reality of the scientific consensus understanding of anthropogenic global warming—or what shall be referred to herein as anthropogenic climate disruption (ACD). However, as is made clear below, this is not a book about climate science: This is a presentation of the results of analysing why some people dispute the reality, reliability or reasonableness of this science.

This book is based on research originally undertaken—and a dissertation written—as part of my MA in Environmental Politics from Keele University in Staffordshire (in 2010-11). As such, it was entitled *A discourse analysis of climate change scepticism in the UK*, wherein 'discourse analysis' was understood in the sense proposed by John Dryzek (2005)—analysing the things people say for the following: (a) basic entities recognised or constructed; (b) assumptions about natural relationships; (c) agents and their motives; and (d) key metaphors and rhetorical devices used.

Academics generally disapprove of the publication of academic research via non-academic, non-peer-reviewed routes. However, I am trying to reach more than just an academic audience. Therefore, it is genuinely hoped that in re-working this research for wider publication, I have made it "accessible" to the non-academic and non-technical reader. However, this book retains many of the features of a piece of academic research, such as the way all sources cited are referenced; endnotes (at the end of each chapter where necessary); and a comprehensive bibliography. It also includes an Appendix, which provides additional context and discussion of many of the key quotations referred to in the main text.

As a piece of social science research, no attempt was made to prove or disprove the validity of the scientific consensus that climate change is happening and that human activity is its primary cause. However, this reality was assumed solely in order to analyse the views of climate change sceptics who dispute it. To this end, the following are summarised herein: the philosophical roots of scepticism; its possible misappropriation for ideological reasons; and the psychological causes of denial. One of the key foundations of this work is the conclusion reached by a variety of researchers that conservative think-tanks (CTTs) often act as the primary driving force of campaigns to deny environmental problems. Accordingly, the output of such UK-based CTTs is analysed, along with that of scientists, economists, journalists, politicians and others. The findings of this research may be summarised as follows:

Whereas the majority of CTTs examined dispute the existence of a legitimate consensus and the majority of sceptical journalists focus on conspiracy theories, the majority of scientists and economists equate environmentalism with a new religion. For their part, politicians and others analysed appear equally likely to cite contrarian and/or economic arguments for inaction. However, because of the economic and political realities of the world in which we live, politicians will not take any action that will be unpopular with business interests and/or the wider electorate. If this is the case, Peter Jacques (2009) would appear to be right to conclude that anti-environmentalism (i.e. environmental scepticism) needs to be exposed as being "in violation of the public interest".

Therefore, as suggested in an editorial in the *Independent* newspaper on 8 July 2010, "The most important message to emerge from the three [so-called 'Climategate'] inquiries is that there is no evidence whatsoever to support the view that climate scientists set out to manipulate or falsify data in order to boost the case for climate change . . . We should not be distracted any further from formulating effective policies to deal with it."

I am grateful to staff at Keele University for their guidance in the preparation of this work, in its original form, although the views expressed herein are entirely my own. I should also wish to acknowledge the significance of certain publications in prompting me to choose this research topic (*Merchants of Doubt* [2010] by Naomi Oreskes and Erik Conway); to realise its importance (*Requiem for a Species* [2010] by Clive Hamilton); and to appreciate its proper context (*Environmental Skepticism* [2009] by Peter Jacques). Without them, my dissertation would never have been (respectively) conceived, pursued, and completed.

On a more general note, I should wish to acknowledge the tireless efforts of non-sceptical journalists such as George Monbiot, whose efforts to promote wider understanding of environmental issues have done so much to bring climate change to the fore as the most important issue of our time.

List of Abbreviations

ACD	Anthropogenic Climate Disruption
AERF	Atlas Economic Research Foundation (Atlas Network)
AOSIS	Alliance of Small Island States
APHG	Associate Parliamentary Health Group
APS	American Physical Society
ASI	Adam Smith Institute
BBC	British Broadcasting Corporation
CDA	Critical Discourse Analysis
CMD	Centre for Media and Democracy
CO_2	Carbon Dioxide
CPS	Centre for Policy Studies
CR	Climate Realists (website)
CRU	Climate Research Unit
CTT	Conservative Think Tank
DUP	Democratic Unionist Party
E&E	Energy and Environment (journal)
EA	Environment Agency
EU	European Union
FFL	Fossil Fuel Lobby
GHG	Greenhouse Gas
GWPF	Global Warming Policy Foundation
HI	Heartland Institute
IEA	Institute of Economic Affairs
IOP	Institute of Physics
IPCC	Intergovernmental Panel on Climate Change
IPN	International Policy Network
ISBN	International Standard Book Number
LJMU	Liverpool John Moores University
MIT	Massachusetts Institute of Technology
NSW	New South Wales
OECD	Organisation for Economic Co-operation and Development
OPEC	Organization of the Petroleum Exporting Countries
RCP	Revolutionary Communist Party
RMS	Royal Meteorological Society

SA	Scientific Alliance
SBC	Sonja Boehmer-Christiansen
SEPP	Science and Environmental Policy Project
SPPI	Science and Public Policy Institute
SW	Source Watch
TMT	Terror Management Theory
UEA	University of East Anglia
UNFCCC	United Nations Framework Convention on Climate Change
US(A)	United States (of America)
WA	Weather Action
WMO	World Meteorological Organisation
WV	Water Vapour
WWF	World Wildlife Fund

Introduction

Choice of Topic

The subject of climate change is rarely out of the news today: whether that be as a result of the apparently-increasing frequency of extreme weather events of all kinds; or the publication of some new research findings relating to flowering plants, migratory birds, or the melting of permafrost, glaciers, and/or sea ice. Therefore, with regard to the latter, it may be pertinent to repeat a comment made by the NASA climate scientist Jay Zwally, as reported in the *New York Sun* newspaper on 12 December 2007:

> "The Arctic is often cited as the canary in the coal mine for climate warming. Now, as a sign of climate warming, the canary has died. It is time to start getting out of the coal mines" (Borenstein 2007).

In the second edition of *The Rough Guide to Climate Change*, Robert Henson has summarised what he calls the "climate change contrarian"[1] position in the following way:

> The atmosphere may not be warming; but if it is, this is probably due to natural variation; but if it isn't, the amount of warming is probably not significant; but if it is, the benefits should outweigh the disadvantages; but if they don't, technology should be able to solve problems as they arise; but if it can't, we shouldn't wreck the economy to fix the problem (*after* Henson 2008: 257).

In isolation, this has the appearance of a so-called "straw man" argument. However, not only does Henson admit that no single "contrarian" believes all of these things (ibid: 258), he then goes on to spend several pages summarising the scientific consensus view that negates each proposition in turn (ibid: 258-66).

With regard to the last of these propositions (i.e. the economic argument for not taking action), it may be significant to note that in the *Stern Review: The Economics of Climate Change*, Sir Nicholas Stern pointed out that our failure to deal with the causes of climate change may well be ". . . the greatest market failure in history" (2006: 1).

Thus it is possible that *The Stern Review* has been highly influential in prompting the UK Government, unlike that in the US, to adopt a proactive approach to tackling climate change. However, despite the likely adverse consequences (both environmental and economic) of any delay in taking action, it is arguable that progress continues to be impeded by those who would dispute the regulatory and scientific consensus; both here and in the US.

Furthermore, although the debate as to whether or not human (anthropogenic) activity is the primary cause of this climate change is well documented in the United States of America, based on the findings of preliminary research for the dissertation on which this book is based, the same cannot be said for the UK. For example:

- Both *Betrayal of Science and Reason* by Paul and Anne Ehrlich (1996) and *Merchants of Doubt* by Naomi Oreskes and Erik Conway (2010) are American publications that barely acknowledge the existence of the rest of the world.[2]
- Globally, there are literally dozens of organisations promulgating climate change scepticism; but they are nearly all based in the USA.
- Whereas there are literally dozens of potentially key individuals in the US similarly involved,[3] they are far fewer in number in the UK.

This may be one reason why the proportion of the US population that believes that we humans are changing the climate recently fell from 87% to 75% (Live Science 2010). What may be more surprising is that the equivalent figure for the UK population appears to be lower—at 70% (Dept for Transport 2010: 8). However, an equivalent figure for Earth Scientists is 82%; and for Climate Scientists it may even be as high as 97% (Le Page 2007).

However, in a modern representative democracy, governments need a mandate to act (e.g. Carter 2007: 358-9); whereas in the kind of participatory democracy that many environmentalists would prefer, action (to mitigate avoidable climate change) requires the majority of the population to be motivated to seek change (e.g. Smith 2003: 53-5). Furthermore, in *Requiem for a Species: Why we resist the truth about climate change*, Clive Hamilton reluctantly concludes that the most likely means to the required end of getting governments to take action will be widespread civil disobedience (2010a: 225).

Therefore, although scientific scepticism is healthy, widespread rejection of scientific authority is dangerous because, either way, it is likely to inhibit necessary action being taken. However, since 'Climategate',[4] it would seem that such corrosive anti-scientific rhetoric has become even more visible and strident. Indeed, in *Merchants of Doubt*, Oreskes and Conway demonstrate that (in the US at least) this scepticism is actually being orchestrated by right-wing libertarian organisations with a vested interest in the maintenance of "business as usual".

If so, this is very dangerous indeed because residual scientific uncertainty has been turned into unreasonable public doubt, thereby inhibiting the progress on international agreement necessary to ensure collective action is taken to mitigate the effects of what is almost certainly a very serious global problem.

However, this book is effectively the summary of academic research; not a demand for action on climate change. Therefore, although it is necessary to summarise the scientific consensus in order to delimit what it is that sceptics wish to "deny, downplay, or dismiss" (Wikipedia 2011a), care has been taken to do this in an objective fashion; so as to avoid any potential accusation of confirmation bias (i.e. setting out to find evidence for a theoretical position already held).

In light of all of the above, this discourse analysis was focussed on the UK.[5]

Definitions

For the avoidance of any doubt, the key terms shall be understood as follows (with more detail provided in the subsequent theoretical **Background** chapter of this book).

Discourse Analysis

From a social constructivist perspective, Phillips & Jørgensen cite Vivien Burr's four premises for discourse analysis (i.e. that knowledge (1) is not objective truth; is influenced by (2) history and culture; and (3) by social interaction; and (4) determines any consequential social action) as being common to their three proposed approaches to discourse analysis; namely discourse theory, critical discourse analysis, and discourse psychology (Phillips & Jørgensen 2002: 5).

In *The Politics of the Earth*, John Dryzek proposed that discourse analysis should involve assessing (a) basic entities recognised or constructed; (b) assumptions about natural relationships; (c) agents and their motives; and (d) key metaphors and rhetorical devices used (2005:19). This is the approach adopted herein, which may be called Dryzekian. It would also appear to be most-closely allied to Phillips &

Jørgensen's "discourse psychology". As such, facets (a) to (c) of Dryzek's approach may include belief in conspiracy theories; which will be highlighted where explicitly stated (i.e. elaborated upon in *A brief history of discourse analysis* below).

Climate Change Scepticism

Using Henson's description of those he calls "contrarians", climate change scepticism is deemed to encompass a variety of views; ranging from denial that change is occurring (and/or that human activity is the primary cause) to those that believe "we shouldn't wreck the economy to fix the problem". Furthermore, where the context permits a distinction to be made between natural climate variability and change now attributed to artificially increased greenhouse gas (GHG) emissions, anthropogenic climate disruption shall be abbreviated to ACD herein.

Where Henson uses the term "contrarian", the term climate change "denier" is often used in a pejorative sense by those seeking to present their opponents as being deceitful, intellectually dishonest, and/or irrational (cf. holocaust deniers; creationists; and/or "flat earthers").

Therefore, the term "climate change denier" is avoided herein because of the pejorative way it is often used, even though there would appear to be quite a variety of things that are actually denied (or questioned) by the sceptics. However, in this context, some observers have even questioned use of the term "sceptic" (or "skeptic" if American)[6] on the basis that, instead of disavowing knowledge or belief, people so labelled dispute unwelcome facts for ideological reasons. Since the legitimacy of such criticism is fundamental to the conclusions that may be drawn from this research, it is considered essential to outline the history of scepticism *per se* that lies behind such a critique (see *The philosophical roots of scepticism* below).

Purpose of research

Given all of the above, the basic question to be addressed herein is as follows: What are the most common discourses (arguments adopted, rhetorical devices and metaphors used, and conspiracy theories invoked) by climate change sceptics; how are these distributed amongst differing groups (i.e. organisations, scientists, economists, journalists, politicians, and others); and what (if anything) does this tell us about their motives?

Methodology adopted

This is a case study of climate change scepticism in the UK: It has involved theory testing—searching for evidence of bias on the part of those promoting climate change scepticism. This has been achieved by means of documentary research of (mainly) primary and secondary sources, including the following:

- Websites of corporate bodies;
- Scientific articles and opinion pieces published by individuals; and
- Biographical and autobiographical literature on key individuals.

The remainder of this book therefore comprises the following:

- a chapter providing the theoretical **Background** to discourse analysis, scepticism and denial; as well as an analytical framework for this research.
- six separate chapters looking at the key **Organisations**, **Scientists**, **Economists**, **Politicians**, **Journalists**, and **Others** in the UK promulgating sceptical ideas. As such, each chapter includes three elements, as follows:

    i. An outline of the preliminary research undertaken (which determined what was to be analysed);

ii. A summary of the documentary evidence examined and the key findings of the analysis undertaken; and
   iii. A tabulated and statistical summary of those findings.

- a **Discussion**, which contextualises the analysis of each group by drawing on; and—where necessary—elaborating upon the issues raised in the theoretical 'Background' chapter.
- a **Summary**, which brings together the tabulated/statistical analysis for each of the groups analysed; and discusses differences that can be seen and/or patterns in the data.
- **Conclusions** arising from all of this research.

Notes on Chapter 1—Introduction

[1] This presupposes the existence of a scientific consensus view that climate change is happening and that human activity is the primary cause of it. As a work of social science, the purpose of this research is not to prove or disprove the validity of this consensus. Its existence is taken as given, however, in order to examine those views that diverge from it.

[2] See: *The political misappropriation of scepticism* in the **Theoretical Background** chapter herein.

[3] In September 2005, former US Vice President Al Gore said . . . "Two thousand scientists, in a hundred countries . . . have produced . . . a consensus that we . . . face a string of terrible catastrophes unless we act to prepare ourselves and deal with the underlying causes of global warming" (Gore 2005). Whereas, in July 2003, Republican Senator James Inhofe said . . . "With all of the hysteria, all of the fear, all of the phony science, could it be that man-made global warming is the greatest hoax ever perpetrated on the American people? It sure sounds like it" (Inhofe 2003). Unfortunately, they cannot both be right.

[4] The illegal disclosure of University of East Anglia/Climate Research Unit (UEA/CRU) emails and data in November 2009 is widely regarded as having contributed to the failure to reach significant agreement at the UNFCCC Meeting in Copenhagen the following month.

[5] However, because the organisations and/or individuals identified are often referred to by their peers in the UK, it may be useful summarise them here:

Sceptical Organisations and Individuals in the United States of America

Organisations	Individuals
American Petroleum Institute CATO Institute George C. Marshall Institute (GMI) Heartland Institute (HI)	Robert Jastrow, Bill Nierenberg, Fred Seitz, and Fred Singer (founders of GMI). Stephen McIntyre, Ross McKitrick, and Patrick Michaels. Willie Soon and Sallie Baliunas. Richard Lindzen (Environmentalists = "*Climate alarmists*"). Freeman Dyson (Environmentalism = "*New religion*").

N.B. This information is based on the research by Oreskes and Conway (2010) and information from the online encyclopaedia *Wikipedia* website.

[6] Such as David MacKay (2009), Peter Jacques (2009), and Clive Hamilton (2010a). This is discussed further in *The political misappropriation of scepticism* in the **Theoretical Background** chapter herein.

Background

A brief history of discourse analysis

Although Michel Foucault is often cited as the originator of modern discourse analysis, he was primarily concerned with analysing discourse produced in the context of political resistance to establishment efforts to engender subjection, and "against subjectivity and submission" (cited in Macdonell 1986: 19). Acknowledging the potential for confusion over the wide variety of uses of the term 'discourse analysis', Jonathan Potter and Margaret Wetherell suggested this was due to concurrent research in "psychology, sociology, linguistics, anthropology, literary studies, philosophy, media and communication studies" (Potter and Wetherell 1987: 6); and cited Stubbs (1983) and Macdonell (1986) as examples of authors (using the term in linguistic and social science contexts respectively) having no overlap whatsoever; and of Foucault as a "continental" user of the term in a primarily historical context (ibid: 6-7).

As such, this book has a primarily psychological context; in that the research it summarises sought to answer the following question: Is it possible to determine (from what they say alone) why some people continue to doubt something that the majority of scientists have concluded is happening (i.e. ACD)?

In her introduction to *Methods of Critical Discourse Analysis* (CDA), Ruth Wodak suggests that CDA may be defined as fundamentally concerned with analysing opaque as well as transparent structural relationships of dominance, discrimination, power and control as manifested in language. Wodak cites Habermas as having claimed that 'In so far as the legitimations of power relations . . . are not articulated . . . language is also ideological' (Wodak 2001: 2).

By any reasonable measure, climate change sceptics are now a disempowered minority and, therefore, use of CDA would seem inappropriate. However, writing in *Analysing Discourse* in 2003, Norman Fairclough's relational approach to analysing text is more promising, as it distinguishes between analysis of internal and external relations in a body of text: where internal relations include semantics, grammar, and vocabulary; and external relations include actions, identifications, and representations (Fairclough 2003: 36-7).

Therefore, summarising all of this, discourse is essentially any "particular way of talking about and understanding the world" (Phillips & Jørgensen 2002: 1) and, although the term discourse analysis has a number of potentially different meanings, here it is best understood in a social constructivist sense (i.e. the belief that all knowledge is learnt rather than discovered and is therefore socially constructed).

Given all of the above, the Dryzekian approach to discourse analysis (defined in the Introduction) can be seen to be similar to both Fairclough and Phillips & Jørgensen. However, whereas Dryzek's facet (d) is clearly a matter of vocabulary, the others may or may not be a matter of interpretation and, if not clearly stated, may require an assessment of the thinking that lies behind what is written. However, this book does not include assessment of any motives unless they are explicitly stated in the sources (i.e. documents) examined and referenced.

The philosophical roots of scepticism

Arne Naess identifies the origins of ancient scepticism as being the 3rd Century BC Greek philosopher Pyrrho (hence named "Pyrrhonism"), who saw scepticism as the logical end-point of intellectual inquiry; with the mature sceptic still seeking knowledge (because he or she "does not claim to know that truth cannot be found"); and "prepared to investigate and evaluate any new argument in relation to any conclusion"

(Naess 1968: 5-6). It is self-evidently the case that climate change sceptics do not do this.

In *Unnatural Doubts*, Michael Williams focuses on modern Cartesian scepticism (i.e. named after René Descartes), which claims that "there is no such thing as knowledge of the external world" (1991: xii). Williams also suggests that the fundamental question regarding scepticism is whether doubts raised are "natural" and "intuitive". Williams also cites Thompson Clarke as having put the question thus: Are sceptics examining . . . "our most fundamental convictions [about the nature of reality] or the product of a large piece of [their own] theoretical philosophising about empirical knowledge . . . ?" (ibid: 1). Climate change sceptics, it is suggested here, are clearly doing the latter.

In 1996, Timothy Fuller edited and published what he described as a posthumous summary of the thoughts of Michael Oakeshott (1901-1990) on modern politics and government (Oakeshott 1996: vii). In this, scepticism is discussed as a political rather than philosophical entity; with the politics of faith and the politics of scepticism as two masters, poles or extremes ". . . between which [for at least five centuries] our activity of government and our understanding of what is proper to the office of government have fluctuated" (ibid: 21). These two poles are equated with (1) authoritarian control "for the purpose of achieving human perfection" [i.e. utopianism such as that of Karl Marx] (ibid: 24); and (2) government "detached from the pursuit of human perfection" [i.e. a utilitarian approach] (ibid: 31). Therefore, if Oakeshott's differentiation of the politics of faith and the politics of scepticism may be reduced to contrasting idealism and realism, climate change sceptics are clearly pursuing the politics of faith; in that they uphold the idealistic view that ACD is not a real problem.

In 2002, Neil Gascoigne, like many others before him, summarised the sceptical position as one that questions the reality of anything and everything we think we know (Gascoigne 2002: 1). He cited two arguments used by sceptics to generate doubts, namely (1) the "argument from ignorance" [e.g. we cannot prove we are not dreaming]; and (2) the "Agrippan argument" [e.g. a childish retort of "why" in response to any adult statement of fact] (ibid: 6). Indeed, although some climate change sceptics do both of these things in a debating context, this is often to avoid confronting the reality of the weight of scientific evidence arrayed against them. Instead, they seem to favour the existence of an alternative explanation that, they argue, deserves equal consideration (even if it has been repeatedly shown to be erroneous elsewhere).

The political misappropriation of scepticism

In 2000, Timothy Luke cited Germany's Minister of the Environment at the 1992 *Earth Summit* in Rio de Janeiro as having said, 'I am afraid that conservatives in the United States are picking "ecologism" as their new enemy' (Luke 2000: 58).

By 1996, Paul and Anne Ehrlich had become so frustrated with this ideological opposition to environmentalism that they wrote:

> The time has come to write a book about efforts being made to minimize the seriousness of environmental problems . . . by a diverse group of individuals and organizations . . . with differing motives and backgrounds . . . With strong and appealing messages, they have successfully sowed seeds of doubt among journalists, policy makers, and the public at large about the reality and importance of such phenomena as overpopulation, global climate change, ozone depletion, and losses of biodiversity (Ehrlich & Ehrlich 1996: 1).

In 2009, David MacKay produced his widely-acclaimed book, *Sustainable Energy: Without the Hot Air*, investigating options for feasible—yet sustainable—global energy policy. As such, although climate change was not the focus of the book,

MacKay acknowledged that his concern regarding ACD was a major motivating factor. Taking the scientific reality of the greenhouse effect as a given and reflecting on the observed super-exponential growth in atmospheric carbon dioxide concentrations since the industrial revolution, he posed the following questions to any ambivalent reader:

> Does 'sceptic' mean 'a person who has not even glanced at the data'? Don't you think that, just possibly, something may have happened between 1800AD and 2000AD . . . that was not part of the natural processes present in the preceding thousand years? (MacKay 2009: 6).

Peter Jacques suggests that whereas modern philosophical (Cartesian) sceptics disavow the legitimacy of all scientific knowledge (as being solely provisional) and ancient (Pyrrhonian) sceptics disavow all belief (based on either perception or reasoning), climate sceptics do not disavow either knowledge or belief: They reject the consensus view of ACD as "junk science" or "environmental alarmism" because it represents a fundamental moral challenge to our collective failure to decouple environmental degradation from economic growth (Jacques 2009: 1).

Quoting from Luke (2000), Hamilton sees climate change scepticism as rooted in an ideologically-driven need to find a replacement for the 'red menace' (following the collapse of Communism in Eastern Europe)—allied to contempt for "liberal intellectuals who had betrayed the Western tradition with a sustained critique of its assumptions and achievements"—which coalesced into their new 'green scare' (Hamilton 2010a: 98).

Most recently, the publishers of *Merchants of Doubt* (Oreskes and Conway 2010) observed that the US scientific community has "produced landmark studies on the dangers of DDT, tobacco smoke, acid rain, and global warming. But at the same time, a small yet potent subset of this community leads the world in vehement denial of these dangers".[1]

The psychological causes of denial

When Leon Festinger published *A Theory of Cognitive Dissonance* in 1957, he introduced it by citing the example of someone continuing to smoke cigarettes even though they know doing so is bad for them. He also suggested that the discomfort this knowledge causes will make them try to rationalise or justify their behaviour (Festinger 1957: 2). Furthermore, he proposed that when faced with such behavioural inconsistency (i.e. dissonance), which makes them feel uncomfortable, people "will actively avoid situations and information which would likely increase the dissonance" (ibid: 3). Thus, he suggested that cognitive dissonance "can be seen as an antecedent condition which leads to activity oriented toward dissonance reduction just as hunger leads to activity oriented toward hunger reduction" (ibid: 3).

In his 2010 book, *Voodoo Histories: How conspiracy theory has shaped modern history*, David Aaronovitch defines conspiracy theory as "the unnecessary assumption of conspiracy when other explanations are more probable"; which he equates to 'Occam's razor' [i.e. the simplest explanation is most likely to be the true one] (2010: 5-6). He reviews a large number of modern conspiracy theories;[2] and draws a number of conclusions under the title 'Bedtime Story' (which hints at the nature of his overall thesis): We invent conspiracy theories to make ourselves feel better and/or to absolve ourselves of responsibility for things that did not go the way we would have wanted. Conspiracy theories are, in effect, "history for losers" because, if ". . . it can be proved there has been a conspiracy . . . defeat is not the product of . . . [our] inherent weakness or unpopularity [or that of our argument or belief]" (ibid: 326-7).

Therefore, if cognitive dissonance is the cause, confirmation bias (a tendency "to filter information to retain only what conforms to one's preferences, and to reject what does not")[3] is the effect: By being selective in what you read, or who you listen to, you will receive only messages that you want to; ones that enable you to remain "comfortable". You see only what you want to see; and believe only what you want to believe.

Unfortunately, in any large-scale disagreement, people on both sides of an argument will often accuse the other party of confirmation bias. However with regard to any subject—if not climate change in particular—it could be argued that those who reject any or all data that does not fit their world view are likely to be suffering from cognitive dissonance. In recognition of this problem, Hamilton responded to potential criticism of the questions that he thought it reasonable to ask[4] by asserting: "Beginning with the facts makes analysis of the motives of those who reject them fair game" (2010a: 98).

Analytical framework for research

The basic analytical framework for this research was a typology of climate change scepticism adapted from that proposed by Dryzek for Environmental Discourses (see Box 1.1, in Dryzek, 2005: 15), looking at what Peter Newell (2000) called "non-state actors", which were taken to encompass non-governmental organisations and private individuals; including those working for mass-media (i.e. authors and journalists).

It was considered that a quantitative and positivist approach was feasible (i.e. that facts are discoverable from the mission statements of the organisations; and from the backgrounds, affiliations, statements, and publications of individuals involved). Furthermore, it was considered feasible to reduce Henson's caricature of climate change sceptics to four basic sceptical "positions" that may be adopted: These are that ACD is (1) not happening; (2) not significant; (3) not problematic; or (4) not worth fixing. Therefore, adopting a presentational approach similar to Dryzek—but incorporating the above—a potential typology of climate change scepticism is presented in Table 1, below:

Table 1: Proposed Typology of Climate Change Scepticism

	Laissez-faire	Reformist
Prosaic	Contrarianism (1—ACD is not happening)	Economic Rationalism[5] (4—ACD is not worth fixing)
Imaginative	Cornucopianism (2—ACD is not significant)	Prometheanism (3—ACD is not problematic)

It should be noted that, although not fully recognised by Dryzek (2005: 51), a distinction is made here between *Cornucopians*[6] (such as Julian Simon—who do not believe action is yet required to address any anticipated effects of ACD) and *Prometheans*[7] (such as Bjorn Lomborg—who is a prominent proponent of radical technological solutions including environmental stabilisation of the atmosphere by means of geo-engineering).

Notes on Chapter 2—Theoretical Background

[1] See <http://merchantsofdoubt.org/> [accessed 15/06/2011].
[2] For example: those surrounding the Japanese attack on Pearl Harbour in 1941; the assassination of President Kennedy in 1963; and the terrorist attack that destroyed the World Trade Center in 2001.
[3] http://www.businessdictionary.com/definition/confirmation-bias.html [accessed 20/06/2011].

THE DENIAL OF SCIENCE

4   i.e. (1) Why do climate sceptics repudiate the accumulated evidence when it becomes inconvenient; and (2) Why do they *want* the consensus view of the science to be wrong?

5   This is a term defined and discussed by Dryzek (2005: 121-42), but could be synonymous with Karl Marx's "money fetishism" as cited in Elster (1986); and/or Herman Daly's "growthmania" (1974).

6   Named after Cornucopia, the horn of the goat Amalthea in Greek mythology, which Zeus endowed with a supernatural power to provide an unlimited supply of food *etc.* As such, Cornucopians have unlimited confidence in the abundant supply of natural resources; the ability of natural systems to absorb pollutants; and their corrective capacity to mitigate human activities.

7   Named after Prometheus, one of the Titans of Greek mythology, who stole fire from Zeus and so vastly increased the human capacity to manipulate the world. As such, Prometheans have unlimited confidence in the ability of technology to overcome environmental problems.

Organisations

Preliminary research

In 2000, Peter Newell suggested that throughout the UNFCCC process (i.e. since 1992) there have been four non-state actors (the IPCC; the mass media; the fossil fuel lobby (FFL) groups; and the environmental NGOs) exercising varying degrees of influence upon four negotiating blocs of countries (OPEC,[1] USA, EU, and AOSIS[2]). However, overall he stressed the importance of two factors: the FFL backing for OPEC and the USA; and the NGOs backing of AOSIS (Newell 2000: 13-14). This alone is suggestive of an organised campaign being promulgated at an international level to resist any radical policy changes.

With regard to ideologically sceptical organisations, as cited earlier, Oreskes and Conway and Hamilton both suggest that the refusal of sceptics to accept that there is a legitimate scientific consensus view at all is indicative of a desperate attempt to find another truth that they can accept; and, in the process, turn residual uncertainty (since all truth in science is provisional) into unreasonable doubt.

According to research done by a team headed by Peter Jacques, an analysis of sceptical works[3] published between 1972 and 2005 (141 documents) revealed that 92% were authored and/or published by someone with direct links to conservative think tanks (CTTs) (Jacques *et al.* 2008: 349). As a result of this research, Jacques concluded that ". . . environmental scepticism . . . is not just a set of independent rebel scientists . . . the sceptical counter-movement is organised . . . to defend [the status quo] against the environmental movement . . . to stave off changes to globalism" (Jacques 2009: 37).

In the UK, there is no FFL comparable to the former US-based Global Climate Coalition, CTTs seem less prominent, and there is little in the way of existing research-based evidence[4] of a similarly organised sceptical campaign. However, that does not mean that the latter does not exist; and CTTs certainly do exist.

At a book launch for *Requiem for a Species*, Hamilton described the Atlas Economic Research Foundation (AERF)[5] as "one of the more important conduits" between the FFL and CTTs (Hamilton 2010b: 3). The AERF is a not-for-profit organisation based in Washington DC that describes itself as ". . . connecting a global network of more than 400 free-market organizations in over 80 countries to the ideas and resources needed to advance the cause of liberty" (AERF 2011). Their database includes the following 9 organisations based in the UK: Adam Smith Institute (ASI), Centre for Research into Post-Communist Economies, Civitas (The Institute for the Study of Civil Society), E.G. West Centre, Freedom Alliance, Institute of Economic Affairs (IEA), International Policy Network, (IPN), Open Europe, Policy Exchange, Stockholm Network, and the Taxpayers' Alliance.

Of these 9 organisations, the most prominent is arguably the IEA. However, there are other organisations not in the AERF's database that appear to be actively sceptical with regard to climate change.

Key Findings

In 2009, Matthew Sinclair published a report for the Taxpayers' Alliance that was highly critical of the regressive nature of green taxes (falling disproportionately on the poorest in society) but did not actually dispute that ACD is happening (Sinclair 2009: 3-5). Similarly, in 2011, the Policy Exchange has published a report that, although highly critical of UK and EU government policy, is not actually sceptical about ACD: On the contrary, it acknowledges that it is already unlikely that a global average temperature rise of less than 3 to 4 degrees Celsius can now be avoided (Moselle and Moore 2011: 6). Thus, although supported by the AERF, neither organisation would actually appear to be sceptical about ACD.

Therefore, as a result of a literature review and Internet-based research, the most prominent sceptical organisations are identified (in Table 2 below), their discourse summarised, and their scepticism analysed, as follows:

Table 2: Organisations Analysed

Organisation	Title of Document	Reference in Appendix
Adam Smith Institute (ASI)	'About'	ASI (2011)
	'Lord Stern is wrong: giving up meat is no way to save the planet'	Pirie (2009)
Centre for Policy Studies (CPS)	'CPS philosophy'	CPS (2011)
	Foggy science In London'	Singer (2008)
Global Warming Policy Foundation (GWPF)	'History and Mission'	GWPF (2009)
International Policy Network (IPN)	'IPN response to the Royal Society and The Guardian's accusations on IPN's work on Climate Change'	IPN (2006)
Institute of Economic Affairs (IEA)	'About us'	IEA (About us)
	'What we do'	IEA (What we do)
Scientific Alliance (SA)	'About the Scientific Alliance'	SA (2010a)
Weather Action (WA)	'News 35—Climate Fools Day 2010'	WA (2010)

The ASI styles itself as ". . . the UK's leading libertarian think tank" (ASI 2011) and, addressing the *Limits to Growth*[6] argument directly, its President, Dr Masden Pirie (if not the ASI itself) is very clearly Promethean (Pirie 2009).

The CPS ". . . develops and promotes policies to limit the role of the state . . ." (CPS 2011) and gave Dr S. Fred Singer (PhD) a platform from which to propagate his contrarian views (Singer 2008). The CPS would therefore appear to have sided with arguably one of the biggest sceptics of all time (i.e. one of the 4 main players featured in Oreskes and Conway's *Merchants of Doubt*).

According to their website, the GWPF was ". . . launched by economist Lord Lawson and social anthropologist Dr Benny Peiser on 23 November 2009 in the House of Lords—in the run-up to the Copenhagen Climate Summit"—declaring itself to be ". . . open-minded on the contested science of global warming [and] deeply concerned about the costs and other implications of many of the policies currently being advocated . . ." (GWPF 2009). Therefore, whilst being an appeal to reason, this is also a very clear statement of Economic Rationalism (see also the individual analysis of the GWPF's two co-founders in the chapters on **Economists** and **Others** respectively).

The IEA's declared mission is to expound ". . . the role of markets in solving economic and social problems [and] promote the intellectual case for . . . low taxes . . . and lower levels of regulation" (IEA—'About us'). Not surprisingly, perhaps, it is clear that the IEA's focus is to promote the role of market forces in a free society; albeit acknowledging the need for "the efficient use of environmental resources" (ibid). However, this is a very anthropocentric position; one from which even market-based instruments to reduce consumption appear to be excluded by the wording of the remainder of their statements. Therefore, despite the acknowledgement that environmental challenges exist, this remains a very clear statement of the Economic Rationalist position.

In response to an article by David Adam in the *Guardian* newspaper (on 20 September 2006)[7], which identified the IPN as one of a number of organisations being funded by Exxon Mobil, the IPN issued a Press Release suggesting that, in supporting the case for ACD, the Royal Society was going against its own motto *Nullius in verba (wrongly cited as meaning "where is your evidence")*[8]: thereby defending the sceptical argument that the science is not settled; the consensus is not valid; and that debate is therefore still legitimate (IPN 2006).

The SA's mission statement declares that it is concerned ". . . about the many ways in which science is often misinterpreted . . . [and] . . . to promote [supposedly] sound science in the environmental debate" (SA 2010a).[9] From this mission statement, it is not clear where the SA lies with respect to the typology of climate change scepticism proposed herein.[10] However, it features a commonly-implied criticism that ACD is based on flawed science; and is a good example of the way in which sceptics seek to question the intellectual integrity—if not honesty—of the scientific consensus regarding ACD.

WA is an organ of outright denial of ACD: which it conceives as a myth that is not based on evidence; pursued by politicians who have been duped by the proponents of a new religion (WA 2010). WA blames current climate change policy for massive energy price rises & carbon taxes, food price rises, and road deaths on untreated (icy) roads (ibid).[11] Therefore, every single aspect of Henson's caricature of climate change scepticism is featured, but the ultimate message is one of Economic Rationalism—climate change policy is wasting public money and inflicting unnecessary suffering on the population.

Summary

5 out of the 7 organisations cite the absence of a consensus, whereas 4 out of 7 support the economic rationalist "leave it to the market" argument; and 3 out of 7 suggest the ACD problem is not worth fixing. However, in an attempt to seem reasonable, outright denial of the fact that our climate is changing (or that human activity is to blame) is often avoided; although strenuous efforts are made to perpetuate supposedly-legitimate debate.

These findings are summarised in Table 3, below:

Table 3: Research Findings—Organisations

	\multicolumn{7}{c	}{Contrarian}	\multicolumn{4}{c	}{Cornucopian}	\multicolumn{3}{c	}{Economic Rationalism}
	"It's the sun"	"There is no consensus"	"Models are unreliable"	"Temp record is unreliable"	"Antarctica is gaining ice"	Environmental "Alarmism"	New "Religion"	Conspiracy theorist	"Climate's changed before"	"It's cooling"	"It's not bad"	"Technofix" (Promethean)	Not worth fixing	Leave it to the Market	Anti-libertarian
ASI												X		X	
CPS		X											X	X	
GWPF		X											X		
IEA														X	
IPN		X				X	X								
SA		X													
WA	X	X							X				X	X	
Totals	1	5				1	1	1				1	3	4	
Percent	14%	71%				14%	14%	14%				14%	43%	57%	

Notes on Chapter 3—Organisations

1. Organization of the Petroleum Exporting Countries.
2. Alliance of Small Island States.
3. Identified using the content-based ISBN classification system.
4. Apart from Jacques *et al.* (2008).
5. See http://atlasnetwork.org/. Founded in 1981, John Blundell (President of the AERF from 1987 to 1990; and former Director General of the IEA) described its mission as being ". . . to litter the world with free-market think-tanks" (Wikipedia/SourceWatch).
6. Named after the 1972 (Meadows *et al.*) report, produced by a team of researchers at the Massachusetts Institute of Technology (MIT), sponsored by the influential *Club of Rome*; as updated by follow-up reports in 1992 and 2005.
7. See Adam (2006) in references.
8. Although the literal translation is "on the words of nobody", as the Royal Society website explains, this may be taken to mean "take nobody's word for it" [and] "is an expression of the determination of Fellows to withstand the domination of authority and to verify all statements by an appeal to facts determined by experiment" (see <http://royalsociety.org/about-us/history/> [accessed 22/07/2011].
9. However, it should be noted that the terms "sound science" and "junk science" first came to prominence in attempts by tobacco companies to deny the seriously detrimental health effects of long-term cigarette smoking (See Ong, E. & Glantz, S. (2001), 'Constructing "Sound Science" and "Good Epidemiology": Tobacco, Lawyers, and Public Relations Firms' [online], *American Journal of Public Health* 91(11) pp.1749-1757. Available at <http://ajph.aphapublications.org/cgi/content/full/91/11/1749?view=long&pmid=11684593> [accessed 15/06/2011].
10. Given the variety of backgrounds from which its scientific (and non-scientific!) members are drawn, this may be deliberate.
11. Although all of these claims are not entirely without merit, they are, nonetheless, presented in a very prejudicial way, which suggests that it is the politicians (not the entire human race) who are to blame.

Scientists

Preliminary research

Although Jacques has concluded that the environmental sceptic movement ". . . is not just a set of independent rebel scientists . . ." (2009: 37), rebellious scientists definitely do exist. That is to say, although the majority of those that deny the reality of ACD may be non-scientists, some climate change sceptics are nevertheless scientists.

These sceptical scientists have been identified as a result of a literature review and Internet-based research, including reference to the following:

- *Wikipedia*—'List of scientists opposing the mainstream scientific assessment of global warming' (Wikipedia 2011b); and
- *SourceWatch*—a disinformation database, collaboratively published by the Centre for Media and Democracy (CMD), which styles itself as "Your guide to the names behind the news".[1]

Key findings

The documents examined are as summarised below in Table 4 and discussed in the text that follows it.

Table 4: Scientists Analysed

Scientist	Title of Document	Reference in Appendix
Jack Barrett	'Jack Barrett' (SourceWatch)	SW (2009)
	'The Leipzig Declaration on Global Climate Change'	SEPP (1995)
	'Scientific Advisory Forum' (Scientific Alliance)	SA (2010b)
David Bellamy	'Climate stability: an inconvenient proof'	Barrett & Bellamy (2007)
	'Junk Science'	Monbiot (2005)
	'David Bellamy' (SourceWatch)	SW (2011)
	'Manhattan Declaration on Climate Change'	HI (2008)
Piers Corbyn	'Global Warming Debate'	Corbyn (2008)
	'Expect more earthquakes world-wide for next two years'	Corbyn (2011a)
	'Piers says it like it is on Australian Radio'	Corbyn (2011b)
	'Piers challenges CO_2-Warmist "Religion" to come up with evidence at "Climate Week" meeting held in Imperial College'	Corbyn (2011c)
Richard Courtney	Written evidence to the Science and Technology Select Committee	Courtney (2010)
Peter Gill	News 35—Climate Fools Day'	WeatherAction (2010)
	'Climate emails inquiry: Energy consultant linked to physics body's submission'	Adam (2010)
Ian Strangeways	'Issues in Meteorological Observing Networks'	Strangeways (2008)
	Measuring Global Temperatures: Analysis and Interpretation	Strangeways (2009)
	'The Greenhouse Effect: a closer look',	Strangeways (2011)
Graham Stringer MP	'Graham Stringer MP'	APHG[2]
	'Climate change scandal: MPs exonerate professor'	Connor (2010)
	'Parliament misled over Climategate report, says MP'	Orlowski (2010)

26

THE DENIAL OF SCIENCE

Jack Barrett is a chemist, not a climate scientist [see SourceWatch (2009), Scientific Alliance 2010b)]. He is a signatory to the *Leipzig Declaration on Global Climate Change,* which denies the existence of a consensus on the reality of ACD (SEPP 1995). Similarly, David Bellamy is a well-known botanist. He is also a signatory to the *Manhattan Declaration on Climate Change*, which disputes the evidence for ACD and denies that it represents a global crisis (Heartland Institute 2008). Together, Bellamy and Barrettt have disputed the warming effect of CO_2; dismissed *Limits to Growth* as a very distant problem; and questioned the accuracy of all climate modelling (2007).

Piers Corbyn, the founder of WeatherAction and main organiser of *Climate Fools Day*, is an astrophysicist with a life-long interest in meteorology (Wikipedia 2011c). He describes ACD as a "failing theory" and "scientific fraud" (because it supposedly stopped in 1998); maintains it was warmer 1000 years ago; and has made it clear he believes our Sun is the most likely cause of the climatic changes we see (Corbyn 2008). However, he has recently gone much further than this by claiming that:

- solar activity (total radiance, sun-spots, coronal mass ejections, and/or solar flares) can have and is having an effect on plate tectonics (earthquakes and volcanism) (Corbyn 2011a);
- people who believe in ACD are as deluded as [was] Colonel Gaddafi; CO_2 has **no** effect on weather or climate (emphasis added); and that we are heading for a "mini ice age" by 2035 (Corbyn 2011b); and
- ". . . there is no evidence in thousands or millions of years of data that CO_2 changes drive any changes in climate . . ."; and equates acceptance of ACD with religious belief (Corbyn 2011c).

Peter Gill is also a physicist who spoke at *Climate Fools Day* on the subject of "fictitious 'tipping points' and facts about CO_2," (WA 2010). Acting as a Energy consultant (Crestport Services) to the Institute of Physics (IOP), he compiled a highly sceptical submission (e.g. claiming that "Unfortunately, for many people [ACD] has become a religion, so facts and analysis have become largely irrelevant") to the Parliamentary Select Committee investigating the UEA/CRU email scandal (Adam 2010).

Ian Strangeways is a meteorologist who suspects that systematic error (i.e. the urban location of many points of observation—the so-called "heat island" effect) is responsible for apparent warming trends in average global surface temperature data (Strangeways 2008); and that water vapour is far more significant as a GHG than is CO_2 (Strangeways 2009).

Graham Stringer is a Labour MP who had a successful career as a chemist prior to entering Parliament in 1997 (APHG). As the only notable sceptical Labour MP in Parliament (see Preliminary research in Politicians chapter), Stringer was also the only member of the Science and Technology Select Committee to distance himself from its decision to clear Professor Phil Jones (CRU) of any scientific malpractice (Connor 2010). Singer is also quoted as citing excessive cost as reason for not taking action to mitigate ACD (i.e. economic rationalism) on the GWPF website (Orlowski 2010).

Summary

5 out of the 7 scientists equate concern over ACD with a new religion; whereas 4 out of 7 suggest that CO_2 is not the cause of climate change. The same number suggest that pressure to take action to mitigate ACD is politically motivated (i.e. a conspiracy theory); whereas only 2 out of 7 dispute the existence of a legitimate scientific consensus.

These findings are summarised in Table 5, below:

Table 5: Research Findings—Scientists

	Contrarian							Cornucopian				Economic Rationalism		
	"It's the sun"	"There is no consensus"	"Models are unreliable"	"Temp record is unreliable"	"Antarctica is gaining ice"	Environmental "Alarmism"	New "Religion"	Conspiracy theorist	"Climate's changed before"	"It's cooling"	"It's not bad"	"Technofix" (Promethean)	Not worth fixing	Leave it to the Market	Anti-libertarian
Jack Barrett	X	X	X				X								
David Bellamy	X	X			X		X				X				
Piers Corbyn	X						X	X	X	X					
Richard Courtney							X	X							
Peter Gill							X	X							
Ian Strangeways	X			X											
Graham Stringer									X					X	
Totals	4	2	1	1	1		5	4	1	1	1		1		
Percent	57%	29%	14%	14%	14%		71%	57%	14%	14%	14%		14%		

Notes on Chapter 4—Scientists

[1] Wherein CMD elaborates as follows: ". . . *SourceWatch* profiles the activities of front groups, PR spinners, industry-friendly experts, industry-funded organizations, and think tanks trying to manipulate public opinion on behalf of corporations or government" (SourceWatch 2010).

[2] Associate Parliamentary Health Group.

Economists

Preliminary research

Much of what follows is an analysis of the content of a single (IEA) publication in 2008, contributed to and compiled and edited by Colin Robinson, namely *Climate Change Policy: Challenging the Activists*, which (unless indicated otherwise) contains the following biographical information regarding the contributing authors:

- **Sir Ian Byatt** is a former head of the Public Sector Economic Unit and Deputy Chief Economic Advisor within HM Treasury and Director-General of Water Services (Ofwat) from the privatisation of the Water Authorities in 1989 up to 2000.
- **David Henderson** is a former head of the Department of Economics and Statistics within the Organisation for Economic Co-operation and Development (OECD) and Visiting Professor at the Westminster Business School in London.
- **Russell Lewis** is "a veteran campaigner for political and economic freedom who has always been ready to defy majority opinion". In 2007, via the IEA website, he published *Global Warming: False Alarms* (also discussed below), which indicates that Lewis is also a former (Acting) General Director of the IEA itself.
- **Julian Morris** left the IEA to set up the International Policy Network (IPN) in 2001; is the IPN's President and former Executive Director; and has Masters Degrees in Economics and Environment and Resource Economics (IPN 2010).
- **Alan Peacock** is a former Chief Economic Advisor to the Department of Trade and Industry, who holds

THE DENIAL OF SCIENCE

honorary appointments as Professor of Economics at the Universities of York and Herriot-Watt (Edinburgh).
- **Colin Robinson**, a member of the IEA's Academic Advisory Council, is a former business economist within the oil industry who became Chair of Economics at the University of Surrey in 1968, where he is now Emeritus Professor.

From this, it is evident that the same economists appear to move from one CTT to another (sometimes even internationally); and they also repeatedly refer to each other's work (rather than to peer-reviewed science) in order to legitimise their conclusions. This point is elaborated upon in the Discussion chapter.

Key findings

The documents examined are as summarised below in Table 6 and discussed in the text that follows it.

Table 6: Economists Analysed

Economist	Title of Document	Reference in Appendix
Roger Bate	*Global Warming: Apocalypse or Hot Air*	Bate & Morris (1994)
Ian Byatt	'Weighing the present against the future: the choice, and use, of rates of discount in the analysis of climate change'	Byatt (2008)
David Henderson	Governments and climate change issues: questioning the consensus'	Henderson (2008)
Russell Lewis	'Global Warming: False Alarms'	Lewis (2007)
	'Global Alarmism'	Lewis (2008)
Lord Lawson	*An Appeal to Reason: A cool look at global warming*	Lawson (2008)
	An Appeal to Reason: A cool [etc] (paperback edition)	Lawson (2009)
Alister McFarquhar	'Alister McFarquhar'	De-Smog Blog
Julian Morris	'Which policy to address climate change'	Morris (2008)
Alan Peacock	'Climate change, religion and human freedom'	Peacock (2008)
Colin Robinson	'Climate change and the market economy: introduction'	Robinson (2008a)
	'Climate change, centralised action and markets'	Robinson (2008b)

In 1994 Roger Bate and Julian Morris argued that ACD was an artefact of the "heat island" effect; that ACD was a "highly debateable theory" whose effects may well be beneficial (Bate & Morris 1994: 26-7); and cited promethean and economic arguments for inaction (ibid: 42, 47).

Ian Byatt's contribution to Robinson's publication is simply a critique of the very low discount rate used in the *Stern Review*, which Byatt claims (2008) results in gross under-estimation of the real costs of proposed actions to mitigate ACD (see the Appendix for additional content and context).

David Henderson appears to concede that the climate is changing (as it has done before) but that the magnitude of the problem has been overstated (i.e. conspiracy theory) and, therefore, that no radical action is required (Henderson 2008: 72, 73, 75).

Nigel Lawson (former Chancellor of the Exchequer—now Lord Lawson of Blaby)—published his *Appeal to Reason* in hardback (2008) and in paperback (2009) with an additional *Afterword* (but otherwise unchanged). The book contains a wide range of sceptical arguments, but the 2009 *Afterword* (responding to his critics) highlights what he considers (despite his self-acknowledged scientific illiteracy) to be the "three greatest lies": (1) that the science is certain and settled; (2) that global warming is actually happening; and (3) that carbon dioxide is a pollutant (Lawson 2009: 107).

Russell Lewis is clearly a fan of the argument that ACD is a false alarm: He considers that current concern is as flawed as that in the 1970s over an approaching ice age (2007: 5-7) and believes that prominent theologians, politicians, and philosophical scientists have all been duped by what he cites author Michael Crichton has having termed "a kind of fundamentalist religion" (2008: 40).

Alister McFarquhar is an economist, with links to the ASI and is a signatory to the *Manhattan Declaration on Climate Change*, who does not mind being wrongly identified as a climate scientist by numerous CTTs: He is often cited for disputing the consensus; suggesting that CO_2 is not a pollutant; and claiming that climate change is natural (De-Smog Blog).

Julian Morris (IPN) uses very similar arguments to dispute the reality of a legitimate scientific consensus that ACD is actually happening; and to support the view that environmentalism is a new religion (Morris 2008: 132). Conversely, Alan Peacock uses religious-sounding rhetoric to reach the conclusion that ACD is an anti-libertarian conspiracy (Peacock 2008: 114, 130).

The view that environmental alarmism has some of the characteristics of a new religion is one that Robinson highlights in his introduction to his 2008 IEA publication; one that he considers to be dangerous precisely because it challenges the status quo and the sensibility of "business as usual" (2008a: 20-1). In his second contribution to the collection of essays, he also criticises modelling/forecasting as inherently unreliable; saying that any predictions must be treated with scepticism in the light of previous false alarms (2008b: 42, 66).

Summary

5 out of the 9 economists equate concern over ACD with a new religion; whereas 4 out of 9 suggest that pressure to take action to mitigate ACD is politically motivated (i.e. a conspiracy theory); and/or that ACD is a problem that is not worth fixing. Although only a limited sample, it would appear that economic critics of action on climate change prefer to invoke the supposed irrationality of concern over ACD, rather than engage in rational debate over the highly-probable scientific reality of ACD; or the equally-likely political necessity of taking mitigating action to avoid unprecedented environmental changes.

These findings are summarised in Table 7, below:

Table 7: Research Findings—Economists

	Contrarian							Cornucopian				Economic Rationalism		
	"It's the sun"	"There is no consensus"	"Models are unreliable"	"Temp record is unreliable"	"Antarctica is gaining ice"	Environmental "Alarmism"	New "Religion"	Conspiracy theorist	"Climate's changed before"	"It's cooling"	"It's not bad"	"Technofix" (Promethean)	Not worth fixing	Leave it to the Market	Anti-libertarian
Roger Bate			X									X	X	X	
Ian Byatt													X		
David Henderson	X							X						X	
Lord Lawson							X	X	X	X	X		X		
Russell Lewis							X	X	X						
Alister McFarquhar	X	X				X						X			
Julian Morris	X		X				X								
Alan Peacock							X								X
Colin Robinson				X		X	X	X					X	X	X
Totals	3	1	2		2	2	5	4	2	1	2	1	4	3	2
Percent	33%	11%	22%		22%	22%	56%	44%	22%	11%	22%	11%	44%	33%	22%

Journalists

Preliminary research

George Monbiot is probably one of the most well-known environmental journalists in the UK today. He is also the widely-acclaimed author of many books, a veteran environmental protestor, campaigner, and lobbyist. He has held a variety of visiting fellowships in academia and has been awarded a number of honorary doctorates by prominent universities in the UK (Monbiot.com).

He keeps a keen eye upon the output of high-profile sceptics (or all types) and, unlike that of many of his peers, his writing is generally founded on peer-reviewed scientific literature and well-referenced. Of particular note is his 'Top 10 climate change deniers' (Monbiot 2009). As such, his blog and *Guardian* column were therefore the starting point for the research discussed below (and elsewhere herein).

Conversely, the writing of his sceptical colleagues is often highly opinionated and/or controversial (probably deliberately so) and not well-referenced to primary sources of information. However, it is difficult to under-estimate their influence upon public opinion (given that they are often quoted on television by politicians and to scientists). Some of the most influential figures in this arena are discussed below:

Key Findings

The documents examined are as summarised below in Table 8 and discussed in the text that follows it.

Table 8: Journalists Analysed

Journalist	Title of Document	Reference in Appendix
Christopher Booker	*The Real Global Warming Disaster: Is the Obsession with 'climate Change' Turning Out to be the Most Costly Scientific Blunder in History?*	Booker (2009)
	'The climate change scare is dying, but do our MPs notice?'	Booker (2010a)
	'Cancun climate conference: the warmists' last Mexican wave'	Booker (2010b)
James Delingpole	'Climategate: the final nail in the coffin of Anthropogenic Global Warming?'	Delingpole (2009)
	'Never mind the Climategate whitewash—what about our new £50 billion annual climate bill?'	Delingpole (2010)
	Meet the Climate Sceptics' [YouTube video of interview in BBC *Horizon* programme]	Delingpole (2011)
Martin Durkin	'The revolution has been televised'	Monbiot (1997)
	'Complaints & Interventions Report for "Against Nature"'	Ofcom (1998)
	'Broadcast Bulletin', issue number 114 (21 July 2008)	Ofcom (2007)
Andrew Montford	*Hockey Stick Illusion: Climategate and the Corruption of Science*	Montford (2010a)
	'The Climategate Inquiries'	Montford (2010b)
Brendan O'Neill	'About Spiked'	Spiked (2011)
	'Global warming: the chilling effect on free speech'	O'Neill (2006)
	'The icy grip of the politics of fear'	O'Neill (2011a)
	'The persecution of Johnny Ball and how gross intolerance is crushing free debate on climate change'	O'Neill (2011b)
Melanie Philips	'The changing face of Melanie Phillips'	Beckett (2003)
	'The global warming con-trick'	Phillips (2002a)
	'Wet, but not the end of the world'	Phillips (2002b)
	'The global warming fraud'	Phillips (2004)
	'Our political landscape'	Phillips (2008)
	'The deep green fear of the human race'	Phillips (2009)
	'Biography'	Phillips (2010)
Tim Worstall	'About'	Worstall (2007)
	'Tim Worstall's Chasing Rainbows'	ASI (2010)
	'Chasing Rainbows by Tim Worstall'	Independent Minds (2010)

Christopher Booker is a veteran journalist who has written a regular column for the *Sunday Telegraph* newspaper since 1990 (Wikipedia 2011d). In November 2010, Booker concluded an article entitled 'The climate change scare is dying, but do our MPs notice?' by making it clear that he does not accept the findings of 3 UEA/CRU inquiries and, instead, continues to believe that scientists are motivated by concern over securing research funding (Booker 2010a). A month later, in a typically sarcastic[1] article, Booker ridiculed the concept of ACD given the extremely cold weather then gripping the UK; and dismissed geoengineering solutions to the problem as ". . . one of the greatest collective flights from reality in the history of the human race" (2010b). However, in 2009, Booker explained the provenance of his scepticism—having been heavily influenced by Fred Singer's belief that climate change is natural and, therefore, that ACD is a false alarm (Booker 2009: 353-5).

James Delingpole is an author of several books and a regular contributor to the *Times*, *Daily Telegraph*, and *Spectator*, who describes himself as a "libertarian conservative" and as having been "reasonably good friends" with David Cameron and Boris Johnson while at Oxford, where he graduated from Christ Church College with a degree in English Literature in the mid 1980s (Wikipedia 2011e). However, Delingpole is perhaps best known for being the person to label the UEA/CRU scandal "Climategate"; bringing it to the attention of the mainstream media on 20 November 2009 (Delingpole 2009).[2]

Martin Durkin has a history of being sceptical; and for being criticised for making misleading television programmes (Ofcom 1998, 2007): He was the director of Channel 4's *The Great Global Warming Swindle* documentary first broadcast in 2007 and, before that, *Against Nature* in 1997, which characterised environmentalist ideology as "unscientific, irrational and anti-humanist" (i.e. presumably ecocentric or misanthropic). However, immediately after *Against Nature* was first broadcast, Monbiot contextualised its message by highlighting links between Durkin, the Revolutionary Communist Party, the

Living Marxism magazine, and the *Spiked* website (Monbiot 1997). Therefore, although his portrayal of ACD as an ideology or a religion was not new, his critique was—and is—unusual because of its extreme left-wing origin (see Brendan O'Neill below).

Andrew Montford is the author of *Hockey Stick Illusion: Climategate and the Corruption of Science* and, according to Wikipedia, is a Chemistry graduate of St Andrews University and a practicing professional Chartered Accountant (Wikipedia 2011f). Montford is a conspiracy theorist *par excellence*, who believes that:

- As far back as 1979, scientists supposedly saw ACD as ". . . a source of funding and influence without end" (Montford 2010a: 21-2).
- As necessity is the mother of invention, the hockey stick graph was the product of a need to make the Medieval Warm Period "disappear" (ibid: 30).
- The 'Climategate' inquiries were all part of a cover-up to provide government with an excuse to tax people more heavily (2010b: 6).

Brendan O'Neill is the editor of the multi-faceted, left-wing, magazine website *Spiked*, which describes itself as, ". . . an independent online phenomenon dedicated to raising the horizons of humanity by waging a culture war of words against misanthropy, priggishness, prejudice, luddism, illiberalism and irrationalism . . ." (*Spiked* 2011). Thus, there are two aspects to O'Neill's critique of those who fear the consequences of ACD: (1) it is misanthropic and regressive; and (2) it is irrational and illiberal (see O'Neill 2006, 2011a, 2011b; and Hamilton 2010a: 113-5).

Melanie Philips is a veteran journalist who spent much of her career working for the *Guardian* but now writes for the *Daily Mail*. She is also the author of several books. Since moving to the *Daily Mail*, she has been a prolific writer of sceptical articles in which she has variously suggested that:

- ACD as "a con-trick" and "a scam"; and that environmentalists are like Nazis (2002a).
- Attacks on sceptics are an anti-capitalist and misanthropic "witch-hunt" (2002b).
- ACD "has little to do with science and everything to do with politics . . ." and ". . . has become big business . . ." (2004).
- "Anyone who endorses [as US Republican Presidential candidate John McCain does] the man-made global warming scam displays an alarming absence of judgment and common sense" (2008).
- Former Friends of the Earth Director, Jonathon Porritt, is "not so much a friend of the earth as an enemy of the human race" (2009).

Tim Worstall is an English writer and blogger, who writes about a variety of topics, but particularly about economics (Wikipedia 2011g). He describes himself as an "Englishman who has failed at many things . . ." who has turned to writing as ". . . the last refuge of many who could make a living no other way" (Worstall 2007). In 2010, he published *Chasing Rainbows: Economic Myths, Environmental Facts*, which examines what we should be doing "to avoid, curtail or adapt to global warming" (Independent Minds 2010). This implies that Worstall believes that ACD is happening but that most prescriptions as to what we should do about it are economically misguided. As such, Worstall is certainly ideologically opposed to market intervention, and may also not actually believe what he calls "the IPCC's science". However, even assuming that he does believe the science, because the *status quo* is not good enough (i.e. we need *more* globalisation and *freer* markets), he is an active Promethean rather than a passive Economic Rationalist.

Summary

5 out of the 7 journalists consider concern over ACD to be politically motivated (i.e. a conspiracy theory); whereas 4 out of 7 suggest that it is a false alarm and/or invoke anti-libertarian arguments in defence of inaction. None of them has a scientific background and some—like James Delingpole—are even content to admit it. Their opinions appear to be informed by transient weather conditions, or by uncritically accepting the output of other sceptical individuals and/or that of CTTs. Therefore, on the basis of this limited analysis, ideologically-driven scepticism seems the most likely cause of their apparent cognitive dissonance.

These findings are summarised in Table 9, below:

Table 9: Research Findings—Journalists

	\multicolumn{7}{c}{Contrarian}	\multicolumn{4}{c}{Cornucopian}	\multicolumn{4}{c}{Economic Rationalism}
	"It's the sun"	"There is no consensus"	"Models are unreliable"	"Temp record is unreliable"	"Antarctica is gaining ice"	Environmental "Alarmism"	New "Religion"	Conspiracy theorist	"Climate's changed before"	"It's cooling"	"It's not bad"	"Technofix" (Promethean)	Not worth fixing	Leave it to the Market	Anti-libertarian
Christopher Booker					X			X	X	X			X		
James Delingpole								X	X						X
Martin Durkin	X					X		X	X			X			
Andrew Montford								X							
Brendan O'Neill					X										X
Melanie Philips			X		X			X							X
Tim Worstall					X								X	X	X	X
Totals	1	1			4	1		5	3	1		2	2	1	4
Percent	14%	14%			57%	14%		71%	43%	14%		29%	29%	14%	57%

Martin Lack

Notes on Chapter 6—Journalists

[1] Sarcasm from Booker may not be particularly surprising given the fact that he was one of the founders of the *Private Eye* magazine in 1961 (Wikipedia).
[2] Initially very sceptical, Delingpole's view has not softened over time. In fact, if anything, he has become even more cynical and suspicious with the passage of time and subsequent events (e.g. Delingpole (2010) [in the Appendix]).

Politicians

Preliminary research

It is a matter of public record that only 3 MPs (all Conservatives) voted against the third and final reading of the Climate Change Bill in October 2008 (Christopher Chope, Peter Lilley, and Andrew Tyrie) and that, on the verge of doing so, Peter Lilley also joked about the fact that it was, at the time, snowing in London (Hansard 2008c: c.838).

Having interviewed chemist (and Labour MP) Graham Stringer, Bryan Appleyard wrote in the *Sunday Times* magazine (on 6 March 2011) that sceptical Labour MPs do exist, although they are unwilling to admit it publicly for fear of being seen as "politically incorrect":

> The Labour MP Graham Stringer was on the select committee that questioned [the CRU's] Dr Philip Jones about his emails. "It was quite a shock," Stringer says. "It was not just the emails, which were probably over the top, but when you look below at what they were actually doing, they weren't doing science." Stringer, a scientist by training, is one of the few [Labour] politicians to come out as a warming sceptic. But there are plenty of closet sceptics. "With Labour MPs, [Stringer continued] it's become more of an issue like racism: 'Of course you're against it, and if you're not, you're not going to be invited to my dinner party'" (Appleyard 2011).

This then explains the distinct lack of on-the-record scepticism from Labour MPs. However, with regard to their Conservative counterparts, the 3 "rebels" are not the only sceptics within their ranks.

Key Findings

Therefore, whilst noting that Stringer was discussed in the earlier chapter on Scientists, the views of the most prominent Conservative sceptics are set out below in alphabetical order, with the documentary evidence analysed summarised in Table 10, as follows:

Table 10: Politicians Analysed

Politician	Title of Document	Reference in Appendix
Graham Brady	'Cameron hit by Tory backlash on environment'	Grice (2009)
Douglas Carswell	'Are Americans ignorant about climate change?'	Blog (29/09/09)
	'BBC and climate change: are we about to see more balanced reporting?'	Blog (12/10/09)
	'Clacton MP in 'climate change' row'	*Clacton Gazette* (2009)
Christopher Chope	House of Commons Debates Volume 481(153)	Hansard (2008b)
Philip Davies	House of Commons Debates Volume 461(106)	Hansard (2007)
	'Cameron hit by Tory backlash on environment'	Grice (2009)
David Davis	'Why this ferocious desire to impose hair-shirt policies?'	Davis (2009)
Daniel Hannan	'Climate change: the case for scepticism'	Hannan (2009)
Roger Helmer	'Speech in European Parliament on 4 February 2009' [transcript]	Helmer (2009)
	'Cameron hit by Tory backlash on environment'	Grice (2009)
Peter Lilley	'Copenhagen Climate Change Conference'	Lilley (2009a)
	'Climate Change: Preparation for the Copenhagen Climate Change Conference'	Lilley (2009b)
	Lilley, P. (2010), 'About Peter'	Lilley (2010)
John Maples	House of Commons Debates Volume 477(106)	Hansard (2008a)
John Redwood	'About John Redwood'	Redwood (2006)
	'The global warming "swindle"'	Redwood (2007)
	'Those climate projections in full'	Redwood (2010)
Andrew Tyrie	House of Commons Debates Volume 477(106)	Hansard (2008a)
Sammy Wilson	'New environment boss "sceptical"'	BBC News (2008a)
	'Wilson row over green "alarmists"'	BBC News (2008b)
	'Sammy Wilson: I still think man-made climate change is a con'	*Belfast Telegraph* (2008)
	'Sammy's Newsletter Column 1 Jan 2011'	Wilson (2011a)
	'Air passenger duty is damaging local economy'	Wilson (2011b)
	'Issues'	Wilson (2011c)
	'Biography'	Wilson (2011d)

Graham Brady disputes the legitimacy of the consensus view that climate change is happening and that we are causing it (i.e. ACD). Consequently, he does not want the economy "destroyed" to fix a problem we may not have (see Grice 2009). Douglas Carswell agrees and, heavily influenced by reading Ian Plimer's book, *Heaven and Earth*, claims that ". . . it was a lot warmer in the middle ages" (as quoted in the *Clacton Gazette* of 23 October 2009).

Christopher Chope, one of the 3 Tory rebels on the Climate Change Bill, cited a report by a firm of accountants that suggested the UK will be responsible for little more than 1% of global GHG emissions by 2050 (Hansard 2008b: c.769). This is blame-shifting—one of Hamilton's maladaptive coping strategies (2010a: 118-33) for those in denial about ACD.[1]

In 2007, Philip Davies described ACD as a "bandwagon" that people have jumped on with "religious zeal"; and said he was as concerned as anyone else about the world our grandchildren will inherit, but opposed to action that "disproportionately affects our economy and the quality of life of the people of this country" (Hansard 2007: c.1020-21). By 2009, his position had changed very little because, as quoted by Andrew Grice in the *Independent* newspaper of 2 December 2009, he was still calling for "proper cost benefit analysis" (he is clearly not a fan of the *Stern Review*) and bemoaning the apparent fact that anyone who urges caution "is completely decried and treated like a Holocaust denier" (Grice 2009).

Writing in the *Independent* newspaper in 2009, David Davis made it clear he believes those who say global warming stopped in 1998; claiming that the problem was not worth the economic cost or the environmental blight inherent in the solutions then being pursued (Davis 2009).

Daniel Hannan seems to enjoy trying to impress people with the breadth of his knowledge by talking about what he calls the German translation of 'cognitive dissonance'

('Weltanschauung')[2], which he claims afflicts those that believe ACD is real (rather than those who deny it). His reasoning being that because they have invested so much time, money, and indeed entire careers in the issue, ". . . the Rio-Kyoto-Copenhagen crowd understandably find it awkward to re-examine their assumptions" (Hannan 2009). However, he also makes it clear he accepts that our climate is changing ". . . although probably not to the degree claimed by some climate change professionals . . ." and resents the fact that his "scepticism" leads some to label him anti-environmental (ibid). Therefore, Hannan sets out his "green" credentials, and cites (non-scientist) Lawson's *Appeal to Reason* as the reason why, despite being a layman unable "to reach a confident view", he has assumed that ACD is a problem that is not worth trying to fix. Unfortunately, because he—as a non-expert—has assumed sceptical and consensus views have equal merit, he is probably being affected by cognitive dissonance himself.

In a speech to the European Parliament on 4 February 2009, Roger Helmer MEP (mis)quoted Christopher Booker as having said that "global warming alarmism is the greatest collective flight from reality in human history"; describing EU proposals as ". . . planning to spend unimaginable sums of money on mitigation measures which will simply not work [that will] deny us the funds we need to address real environmental problems" (Helmer 2009). Furthermore, according to Andrew Grice in the *Independent*, Helmer has even accused the Church of England of having "abandoned religious faith entirely and taken up the new religion of climate change alarmism instead" (Grice 2009).

The Rt Hon Peter Lilley MP (i.e. a former Cabinet Minister in the Thatcher government) is arguably the most forthright and most experienced of Tory sceptics (and the most senior of the 3 Climate Change Bill rebels). He was a successful stockbroker and businessman before entering Parliament and still maintains positions on the board of directors of several large companies (Lilley 2010). As such, although he does not dispute the basic science of ACD, he does dispute what the climate modellers are telling us (Lilley 2009b).

Therefore, irrespective of whether or not Lilley is a sceptic (he claims he is not), he is quite prepared to rely upon sceptical arguments such as those that say temperature reconstructions are flawed (if not faked) and that climate models are unreliable. Indeed, earlier that same year, in a similar debate on 16 July 2009, Lilley had been even more strident in his opposition to the consensus (IPCC) view of climate science:

> . . . I believe that the claims that the scientific evidence is overwhelming and that the debate is ended are incorrect and exaggerated, that the damages supposed to result from rises in the global average temperature are exaggerated, and that the cost of mitigating that rise in temperature is almost certainly understated. (Lilley 2009a).

Lilley clearly does not accept the findings of the *Stern Review* but, the question remains as to exactly from whom, or where, he was getting his information.

John Maples equates climate scientists with doctors in the 1850s by suggesting that the former are "scratching the surface of something that they do not really understand . . ."—and that what they actually say "does not justify any of the apocalyptic visions . . ." described by some demanding mitigating action be taken (Hansard 2008a: c.103).

The Rt Hon John Redwood MP was one of many who has used Durkin's 2007 *Great Global Warming Swindle* documentary to justify his scepticism—along with mentioning melting ice on Mars and suggesting that warming may have some benefits (Redwood 2007). More recently, he has been happy to ridicule scientific projections and question the entire ACD hypothesis on the basis of isolated extremely cold weather events (Redwood 2010); all in a manner very reminiscent of Christopher Booker.

Andrew Tyrie, the third of the Tory rebels, would appear to have opposed the passage of the Climate Change Bill in October 2008 on primarily economic grounds; dismissing concern over ACD as having "an air of unreality" about it and doubting whether most of its projected consequences will ever happen (Hansard 2008a: c.98).

Sammy Wilson is a Democratic Unionist (DUP) MP and member of the Northern Ireland Assembly, where he held the position of Environment Minister from 2008 to 2009—when his scepticism resulted in his being moved to the Ministry of Finance (BBC News 2008a, 2008b and *Belfast Telegraph* 2008). However, this setback has apparently done nothing to blunt his scepticism or his willingness to speak about it (Wilson 2011a, 2011b, 2011c). Wilson is clearly very intelligent, and a very dedicated and successful politician (Wilson 2011d). However, it is difficult to avoid the conclusion that his sceptical views on climate change (including the dismissal of all scientific evidence for ACD) have been prejudiced by his acceptance of the arguments of economic rationalists (i.e. those who consider economics to be more important than the environment and are therefore prejudiced against accepting that ACD is real).

Summary

6 out of these 12 sceptical Conservative politicians claim that they do not accept the legitimacy of the scientific consensus; and the same number say that, if ACD is happening, it is not worth "wrecking the economy" (Henson) to fix the problem; whereas 3 out of 12 suggest that the ACD has stopped.

Given that none of them has a scientific background it would appear legitimate to ask from whom or where they got their information. However, since there is a clear consensus amongst appropriately-qualified scientific researchers, lobby groups (FFL, CTTs); organisations such as WeatherAction; and the sceptical journalists (that act as conduits for such misinformation) would all appear to be implicated. These findings are summarised in Table 11, below:

Table 11: Research Findings—Politicians

	Contrarian							Cornucopian				Economic Rationalism		
	"It's the sun"	"There is no consensus"	"Models are unreliable"	"Temp record is unreliable"	"Antarctica is gaining ice"	Environmental "Alarmism"	New "Religion"	Conspiracy theorist	"Climate's changed before"	"It's cooling"	"It's not bad"	"Technofix" (Promethean)	Not worth fixing	Leave it to the Market	Anti-libertarian
Graham Brady		X													
Douglas Carswell		X		X											
Christopher Chope													X	X	
Philip Davies							X						X		X
David Davis										X			X		
Daniel Hannan	X									X			X		X
Roger Helmer		X				X	X						X	X	
Peter Lilley		X	X	X											
John Maples		X	X			X									
John Redwood		X									X				
Andrew Tyrie													X		
Sammy Wilson	X								X	X		X			
Totals	2	6	2	2	2	2	1	3	1	1	6	2	2		
Percent	17%	50%	17%	17%	17%	17%	8%	25%	8%	8%	50%	17%	17%		

Notes on Chapter 7—Politicians

[1] These are (1) distancing; (2) diversion; (3) blame-shifting; (4) indifference; and (5) wishful thinking.
[2] The literal translation is actually just "worldview".

Others

Preliminary research

This chapter covers those individuals who appeared particularly influential (from the research into organisations and a review of Monbiot 2009), but who did not fit into any of the categories covered in preceding chapters.

Key findings

The documents examined are as summarised below in Table 12 and discussed in the text that follows it.

Table 12: Other People Analysed

Person	Title of Document	Reference in Appendix
Sonja Boehmer-Christiansen	Undated online interview	Spiked
	International Environmental Policy: Interests and the Failure of the Kyoto Process	(2002)
Philip Foster	'Climate sceptics launch campaign to overturn green targets'	Gray (2010)
	While the Earth Endures: Creationism, Cosmology, and Climate Change (2nd ed)	(2010)
Lord Monckton	'Christopher Monckton'	De-Smog Blog
	'Unsound advice'	(2010)
Benny Peiser	'Benny Peiser'	De-Smog Blog
	'Climate fatigue leaves global warming in the cold'	(2011)
Bruno Prior	'Foreword'	(2008)
Stephen Wilde	'The Death Blow to Anthropogenic Global Warming'	(2008)
	'How Gavin Schmidt and Michael Mann almost got it right in 2001'	(2011)

THE DENIAL OF SCIENCE

Sonja Boehmer-Christiansen is an Emeritus Reader in Geography at the University of Hull and has admitted that she likes to challenge conventional thinking (Spiked). In 2002, she co-authored a book that, amongst other things, challenged the assumption that the IPCC represents a legitimate scientific consensus on the reality of ACD (Boehmer-Christiansen & Kellow 2002: 149, 161).

The Rev. Philip Foster is a retired Church of England Minister, who spoke at the *Climate Fools Day* organised by Piers Corbyn and, like Corbyn, is a regular contributor to the CR website. He has also been cited as advocating economic arguments for not taking action to mitigate ACD (Gray 2010). However, the second edition of his recent book possibly presents the fullest picture of his thinking. It appears to be a multi-faceted work of denial within which he concludes that: "It is now firmly fixed in the public psyche that [ACD] is an established fact of science, despite the fact that there is no scientific evidence for it" (Foster 2010: 167).

Christopher Walter Monckton, 3rd Viscount Monckton of Brenchley, is more informally known as Lord Monckton. He is a Classics graduate of Churchill College Cambridge, a former newspaper editor and a hereditary peer: Formerly a member of the Conservative Party, Monckton was briefly the deputy leader of the UK Independence Party in 2010. He served in Conservative Central Office and worked for Margaret Thatcher's Number 10 Policy Unit during the 1980s (Wikipedia 2011h). Not surprisingly perhaps, Monckton is a prolific writer and public speaker. Furthermore, presumably due to his aristocratic status and well-connected position, he is frequently cited by others as a climate change expert, although he is possibly best described as an amateur. Therefore, although the nature of the dissertation on which this book is based—and its original word limit—made a detailed critique of Monckton's pronouncements both inappropriate and impossible, his position may be summarised as follows: He disputes the existence of a consensus and the veracity of a wide-range of the IPCC's pronouncements and predictions (see Monckton 2010 in the Appendix for details). At best he is a Promethean; at worst a multi-faceted Contrarian.

On his old staff page of the Liverpool John Moores University (LJMU) website, Dr Benny Peiser, co-founder of the GWPF, was described as "a social anthropologist with particular research interest in human and cultural evolution. His research focuses on the effects of environmental change and catastrophic events on contemporary thought and societal evolution" (LJMU 2011). Arguably, Peiser has become notorious (amongst climate scientists at least) for challenging research findings published by Naomi Oreskes and then having to retract his criticisms when they were shown to be invalid (De-Smog Blog). Despite this, however, he has continued to maintain that fears over global warming amount to "hysteria" that is now waning due to so-called "issue fatigue" and public cynicism regarding the motives of politicians espousing contentious policies (Peiser 2011).

Bruno Prior is a business man, invited by Robinson to write the *Foreword* to his 2008 IEA publication. In this, Prior makes it clear that he thinks proposed action to mitigate ACD is disproportionate to the threat posed (2008: 12); and that the government is using fear of ACD as a pretext for increased regulation, taxation and control (ibid: 14). Therefore, Prior seems to have gone beyond the 'leave it to the market' mantra of Economic Rationalism—and beyond the objective truth that all scientific understanding is conditional—to embrace the Contrarian position that seeks to convert residual scientific uncertainty into unreasonable doubt; and to deny that the potential costs and consequences for humanity are far greater than those associated with taking action to limit ACD.

Stephen Wilde likes to refer to himself as "a Fellow of the Royal Meteorological Society since 1968". However, he therefore became a Fellow before professional qualifications became a mandatory pre-requisite and is, in fact, a fully-qualified and practicing solicitor. As such, solicitor Stephen Wilde LLB (Hons) is based in Cheshire and is a regular contributor to the sceptical US-based CR website. In 2011, his postings ranked amongst the most-popular on the CR website; suggesting that he is widely cited as an expert by sceptics in cyberspace in general and the blogosphere in particular. From a review of his CR postings, it is clear that:

- He considers ACD to be an example of environmental alarmism; that the sun is the cause of the changes we are seeing; and that therefore the "theory of [ACD] . . . should now die" (Wilde 2008).
- He suggests and/or believes that those who continue to claim ACD is cause for genuine concern are misguided and/or not being sufficiently rigorous to see the intellectual flaws in their own arguments (Wilde 2011).

However, the language he uses is frequently unscientific and prejudicial; and his work rarely (if ever) published in peer-reviewed scientific journals. Furthermore, as a solicitor, it could be argued that he is no better qualified to pronounce on the subject of climate science than is an investigative journalist.

Summary

Despite an absence of appropriate personal expertise, 4 out of the 6 individuals considered here claim that there is no consensus; and/or consider concern over ACD to be misplaced ("alarmism"); and/or that the ACD problem is not worth fixing.

These findings are summarised in Table 13, below:

Table 13: Research Findings—Other People

	Contrarian							Cornucopian				Economic Rationalism		
	"It's the sun"	"There is no consensus"	"Models are unreliable"	"Temp record is unreliable"	"Antarctica is gaining ice"	Environmental "Alarmism"	New "Religion"	Conspiracy theorist	"Climate's changed before"	"It's cooling"	"It's not bad"	"Technofix" (Promethean)	Not worth fixing	Leave it to the Market	Anti-libertarian
Sonja Boehmer-Christiansen		X				X		X							
Philip Foster		X	X	X		X		X					X		
Lord Monckton		X			X					X	X		X	X	
Benny Peiser		X				X							X		
Bruno Prior													X		X
Stephen Wilde	X					X									
Totals	1	4	1	1	1	4		2		1	1		4	1	1
Percent	17%	67%	17%	17%	17%	67%		33%		17%	17%		67%	17%	17%

Discussion

Preamble

In considering potential reasons for our collective failure to act to prevent ACD, a number of authors appear to have been influenced (either implicitly or explicitly) by Ernest Becker's *The Denial of Death* (1973). For example, Aaronovitch proposed that we try to avoid confronting the "catastrophe of indifference" that our individual lives may be of very little significance in the grand scheme of things (2010: 340), whereas Hamilton suggested that ACD "has the smell of death about it" (2010a: 215).

Janis Dickinson elaborates a little more, exploring what she describes as ". . . one of the key psychological links between the reality of global climate change and the difficulty of mobilizing individuals and groups to confront the problem in a rational and timely manner" and—referring to what psychologists call terror management theory (TMT)—she also categorises denial of climate change; denial of human responsibility; and/or immediacy of the problem as **proximal** TMT responses (Dickinson 2009). Furthermore, as referenced here, both Dickinson and Hamilton suggest that other **distal** TMT responses (focussing on maintaining self-esteem or enhancing self-gratification) can be counter-intuitive and counter-productive.

Dickinson summarises the recent work of Tim Dyson by saying that behavioural "response to the threat of global climate change simply does not match its unique potential for cumulative, adverse, and potentially chaotic outcomes" (ibid). However, Dyson is worth quoting directly: ". . . major behavioural change to limit world carbon emissions is unlikely to happen in the foreseeable future" (Dyson 2005: 119); and—because he explicitly links ACD to the *Limits to Growth* argument—as follows: ". . . with respect to global warming and climate change . . . people will only really alter their behavior [sic] with respect to energy use when they experience serious effects from these phenomena for themselves" (ibid: 147).

Organisations

The work of Jacques *et al.* (2008) is a very significant piece of empirical research that implicates US- and UK-based CTTs in the deliberate misinformation campaign also identified by Hamilton (AERF) and by Oreskes and Conway (GMI *etc.*). In prefacing their research, Jacques *et al.* observed that:

> Since environmentalism is unique among social movements in its heavy reliance on scientific evidence to support its claims . . . it is not surprising that CTTs would launch a direct assault on environmental science by promoting environmental scepticism in their efforts to oppose the environmental movement . . . (2008: 353).

Furthermore, based on their findings, they concluded that:

> Environmental scepticism is an elite-driven reaction to global environmentalism, organised by core actors within the conservative movement. Promoting scepticism is a key tactic of the anti-environmental counter-movement co-ordinated by CTTs . . . (ibid: 364).

Jacques has also highlighted the central aim of CTTs as being to cause confusion and doubt amongst the general public, in order to prevent the creation of a popular mandate for change (i.e. achieved, as noted previously, by countering supposedly "junk science" with their "sound science"), which he refers to as the "science trap" (2009: 148).

Based on the findings of the research published in 2008, Jacques therefore concluded that environmental scepticism is a social counter-movement that uses CTTs to provide "political insulation for industry and ideology from public scrutiny"; and that this deliberate obfuscation stems from a realisation that "anti-environmentalism is an attitude that most citizens would consider a violation of the public interest" (2009: 169). However, Jacques does not blame the CTTs for the ecological crisis he feels we face, as they have merely exploited a dominant social paradigm "because neoliberal globalism and its logic are protected from critique" (ibid: 119).

Scientists

C.S. Lewis once famously remarked that Jesus of Nazareth, intending not to leave us with the option of considering him to have been a good moral teacher, must therefore be mad, bad, or God (*Mere Christianity*, 1952). However, with respect to sceptical scientists, it is considered fair to eliminate all 3 of these possibilities. That is to say, it is hereby assumed that they are not reaching irrational conclusions, being deliberately deceitful, or of superior intelligence to those that support the consensus view (that dangerous ACD is really happening). That being the case, it would seem that there is only one remaining alternative: They have approached their assessment of the data with pre-conceived ideas of what they wish to find. In other words, cognitive dissonance motivated them to find evidence to support a required conclusion (i.e. that ACD is not happening or not dangerous).

This is the conclusion reached by Hamilton (2010a: 101), who also gave them the benefit of the doubt by assuming that they are neither irrational nor deceitful. Furthermore, Hamilton—like Paul and Anne Ehrlich and Herman Daly before him—concluded that cognitive dissonance (i.e. the quest for an alternative reality) causes the rejection of any or all science that would tend to challenge the presumed necessity of continuous economic growth (cf. Daly 1992: 2); and that ideologically-prejudiced scientists are then sought out and supported by those with a vested interest in the continuance of "business as usual". An example that supports this hypothesis is the case of the "big oil" Koch brothers in the USA, who, as recently highlighted by Greenpeace, give more money to fund sceptical scientists than does Exxon Mobil:

> . . . denial of climate change is not something based on healthy scientific scepticism and debate: it is manufactured and bears the "Koch" brand. To put their financial commitment into context, from 2005-2008 the Koch brothers pumped in double the amount that even Exxon spent on undermining climate action over the same period" (Greenpeace 2010).

Economists

Overall, the position of the economists reviewed here tends to be that of Economic Rationalism. However, given that the reality of ACD is apparently conceded by most of them, this begs the question why they don't accept that there is a scientific consensus or, at least, why they don't accept what that consensus is telling us. This would appear to lend weight to the argument of those who have suggested that it is Capitalist economics and/or consumerism that is/are the problem—what Daly calls "growthmania" and Hamilton "growth fetishism". Call it what you will, sceptical economists appear to have decided that they cannot afford to allow the IPCC to be right; and therefore grasp hold of any evidence they can find (or that business-funded science gives to them) that may confirm this view. In other words, this is cognitive dissonance leading to confirmation bias generally being presented as Economic Rationalism.

Journalists

Strictly speaking, Andrew Montford is not a journalist, although he is a published author and is the creator of the sceptical *Bishop Hill* blog. With regard to his *Hockey Stick Illusion* book, however, it should be noted that:

- He wrote this after being directed (via Tim Worstall's blog) to Stephen McIntyre's *Climate Audit* blog (Wikipedia 2011f); and
- Whereas neither Montford nor Worstall is a scientist, Canadian mining consultant McIntyre and economist Ross McKitrick are two of the key players in the so-called Hockey Stick (MBH98) Graph[1] controversy.

Therefore, although sceptical journalists rarely identify their sources, this may be indicative of the likely sources of their disinformation.

In a wide-ranging assessment of both conventional and new media, Neil Gavin and Tom Marshall report that, leaving aside the output of individual sceptics, editors have come under pressure since Climategate to give sceptics more exposure. However, referring to the UEA/CRU scandal, they concluded: "The emails, in essence, did not suggest the scientific consensus was fatally flawed, peer-review undermined, or IPCC reports worthy of dismissal. Consequently, if the broadcasters continue to give climate sceptics significant coverage, they will be doing the public a serious disservice, especially in the run-up to the next IPCC report around 2012-2013" (Gavin and Marshall 2011: 8).

Politicians

None of these sceptical Conservative politicians is or was a scientist: If not outright career politicians, they all have either economic or business backgrounds. As such, although no doubt encouraged by sceptical journalists (as above), their opinions seem most clearly influenced by the output of powerful libertarian lobby groups such as the ASI and the IEA. Given the attendance of many at *Climate Fools Day*, Piers Corbyn and/or WeatherAction would also appear to be involved.

In addition, although time has not permitted conclusive research, it would seem likely that lobbying is actively undertaken at an international level (by the big FFL-backed organisations in the USA) via intermediaries such as the GWPF and Lord Monckton. At very least, MPs like Peter Lilley are not above quoting international climate sceptics such as those that rebuked the APS for declaring its support for action to mitigate ACD.

Politicians are human like the rest of us, but their tendency to avoid focussing on the long-term is heightened by their desire to be re-elected (Dyson 129-30); and because they are generally more concerned with safeguarding the interests of big business than those of humanity as a whole (Hamilton 2010a: 223). Hence "climate change represents a failure of modern politics" (ibid); not just ". . . the greatest market failure in history" (Stern 2006: 1).

A great deal of research was done between the 1970s and 1990s into popular reactions to the realisation that governments had been what is euphemistically termed "economical with the truth". In 2007, W. Peter Robinson noted that national surveys in the UK and USA, between 1973 and 1993, showed significant consequential losses of public confidence and significant increases in cynicism and apathy (Robinson 2009: 279-80). However, although made in connection with the UK in the era of Margaret Thatcher, his description of rhetorical political statements is instructive in the present context: "The arguments were mostly formal, sloganized [sic] appeals to authority entirely lacking in any substantial, supportive empirical evidence" (ibid: 277).

Whereas politicians are often criticised for equivocation, their opponents are always very certain about what should be done. By contrast, both parties in any debate (not just in politics) often use rhetorical devices to make statements of opinion appear to be ones of fact. Furthermore, as Peter Bull has pointed out, "[political] and economic ideologies are often framed in metaphorical terms" in the hope that, rather like a magician using diversionary tactics to stop you looking where they don't want you to, "metaphors can conceal as much as they illuminate" and "misleading metaphors can . . . seriously affect our lives" (Bull 2007: 268).

Others

The other people whose discourses have been analysed herein are, by definition, none of the above; but neither are they all the same. Their individual reasons for wanting to deny the reality of ACD are therefore likely to be different and incapable of collective philosophical or psychological assessment. However, in the final analytical chapter of this study (which now follows), the findings of all previous chapters are discussed in the context of the proposed typology of climate change scepticism presented earlier (in Table 1).

Synopsis

Overall, it would appear that many people are undecided, uncertain, and/or confused about who to believe and, therefore, even though the majority of politicians may not be sceptical, it is perhaps not surprising that the UNFCCC process has made such little progress.

This is the conclusion reached by James Hoggan, author of *Climate Cover-up—The Crusade to Deny Global Warming*:

Democracy is utterly dependent upon an electorate that is accurately informed. In promoting climate change denial (and often denying their responsibility for doing so) industry has done more than endanger the environment. It has undermined democracy. There is a vast difference between putting forth a point of view, honestly held, and intentionally sowing the seeds of confusion. Free speech does not include the right to deceive. Deception is not a point of view. And the right to disagree does not include a right to intentionally subvert the public awareness (*De-Smog Blog*—'About the climate cover-up').

Notes on Chapter 9—Discussion

[1] Originally presented in a paper by Michael Mann, Raymond Bradley and Malcolm Hughes in 1998 (i.e. MBH98), this graph featured prominently in the IPCC's Third Assessment Report (AR3) in 2001, since when its authenticity has been repeatedly questioned (by sceptics at least). See <http://en.wikipedia.org/wiki/Hockey_stick_controversy> [accessed 10/06/2011].

Summary

Theoretical Background

The theoretical background to this study comprised the following three elements:

- the philosophical roots of scepticism;
- the political misappropriation of scepticism; and
- the psychological causes of denial.

Analytical Framework

The Analytical Framework (Table 1) was based on the summation of climate change scepticism proposed by Henson (2008: 257). This attempted to differentiate four different positions that sceptics may adopt:

- Contrarianism;
- Cornucopianism (i.e. faith in natural salvation);
- Prometheanism (i.e. faith in technological salvation); and
- Economic Rationalism

Unfortunately, all of the above may actually be forms of denial if they are actually variations of Hamilton's maladaptive coping strategies (distancing; diversion; blame-shifting; indifference; and/or wishful thinking) that seek to downplay, dismiss, or deny the existential threat that ACD poses to continuing human habitation of the planet (at anything like present numbers and/or levels of average standard of living).

Summary of Findings

However, be that as it may, the findings of the Dryzekian discourse analysis (i.e. arguments adopted and rhetoric used), as presented in Tables 3, 5, 7, 9, 11, and 13) above, are all concatenated into Table 14 (on following pages); and then discussed below.

THE DENIAL OF SCIENCE

Table 14: Summary of Discourse Analysis—Argument Frequency

Organisations	Contrarianism										Cornucopianism				Economic Rationalism		
	"It's the sun"	"There is no consensus"	"Models are unreliable"	"Temp. record is unreliable"	"Antarctica is gaining ice"	Environmental "Alarmism"	New "Religion"	Conspiracy theorist	"Climate's changed before"	"It's cooling"	"It's not bad"	"Technofix" (Prometheanism)	Not worth fixing	Leave it to the Market	Anti-libertarian
Adam Smith Institute												X			
Centre for Policy Studies		X											X	X	
Global Warming PF		X											X		
Inst. of Economic Affairs															
International Policy Net.		X					X	X						X	
Scientific Alliance		X							X						
Weather Action	X	X											X	X	
Sub-totals	1	5					1	1	1			1	3	4	
	14%	71%					14%	14%	14%			14%	43%	57%	

Martin Lack

Scientists	"It's the sun"	"There is no consensus"	"Models are unreliable"	"Temp. record is unreliable"	"Antarctica is gaining ice"	"Environmental Alarmism"	New "Religion"	Conspiracy theorist	"Climate's changed before"	"It's cooling"	"It's not bad"	"Technofix" (Prometheanism)	Not worth fixing	Leave it to the Market	Anti-libertarian
Jack Barrett	X	X	X												
David Bellamy	X	X			X		X				X				
Piers Corbyn	X						X		X	X					
Richard Courtney							X	X							
Peter Gill				X			X	X							
Ian Strangeways	X						X	X							
Graham Stringer								X					X		
Sub-totals	4	2	1	1	1		5	4	1	1	1		1		
	57%	29%	14%	14%	14%		71%	57%	14%	14%	14%		14%		

Contrarianism columns: "It's the sun", "There is no consensus", "Models are unreliable", "Temp. record is unreliable", "Antarctica is gaining ice", "Environmental Alarmism", New "Religion", Conspiracy theorist

Cornucopianism columns: "Climate's changed before", "It's cooling", "It's not bad", "Technofix" (Prometheanism)

Economic Rationalism columns: Not worth fixing, Leave it to the Market, Anti-libertarian

THE DENIAL OF SCIENCE

Economists	"It's the sun"	"There is no consensus"	"Models are unreliable"	"Temp. record is unreliable"	"Antarctica is gaining ice"	Environmental "Alarmism"	New "Religion"	Conspiracy theorist	"Climate's changed before"	"It's cooling"	"It's not bad"	"Technofix" (Prometheanism)	Not worth fixing	Leave it to the Market	Anti-libertarian
									Cornucopianism				Economic Rationalism		
			Contrarianism												
Roger Bate				X								X	X	X	
Ian Byatt													X		
David Henderson		X												X	
Lord Lawson								X	X	X	X				
Russell Lewis							X	X	X						
Alister McFarquhar		X	X			X		X							
Julian Morris		X		X			X	X			X				
Alan Peacock							X								X
Colin Robinson						X	X	X					X	X	X
Sub-totals		3	1	2		2	5	4	2	1	2	1	4	3	2
		33%	11%	22%		22%	56%	44%	22%	11%	22%	11%	44%	33%	22%

69

Martin Lack

Journalists	"It's the sun"	"There is no consensus"	"Models are unreliable"	"Temp. record is unreliable"	"Antarctica is gaining ice"	Environmental "Alarmism"	New "Religion"	Conspiracy theorist	"Climate's changed before"	"It's cooling"	"It's not bad"	"Technofix" (Prometheanism)	Not worth fixing	Leave it to the Market	Anti-libertarian
Christopher Booker						X		X	X	X			X		
James Delingpole		X						X	X						X
Martin Durkin							X	X	X			X			
Andrew Montford			X					X							
Brendan O'Neill						X									X
Melanie Philips						X		X							X
Tim Worstall						X						X	X	X	X
Sub-totals		1	1			4	1	5	3	1		2	2	1	4
		14%	14%			57%	14%	71%	43%	14%		29%	29%	14%	57%

THE DENIAL OF SCIENCE

Politicians	"It's the sun" (Contrarianism)	"There is no consensus"	"Models are unreliable"	"Temp. record is unreliable"	"Antarctica is gaining ice"	"Environmental Alarmism"	"New Religion"	Conspiracy theorist	"Climate's changed before" (Cornucopianism)	"It's cooling"	"It's not bad"	"Technofix" (Prometheanism)	Not worth fixing (Economic Rationalism)	Leave it to the Market	Anti-libertarian
Graham Brady		X													
Douglas Carswell		X		X											
Christopher Chope													X	X	
Philip Davies							X						X		X
David Davis										X			X		
Daniel Hannan	X									X			X		
Roger Helmer		X				X	X						X	X	X
Peter Lilley		X	X	X											
John Maples		X	X			X									
John Redwood		X									X				
Andrew Tyrie													X		
Sammy Wilson	X								X	X		X			
Sub-totals	2	6	2	2		2	2		1	3	1	1	6	2	2
	17%	50%	17%	17%		17%	17%		8%	25%	8%	8%	50%	17%	17%

Martin Lack

	It's the sun	There is no consensus	Models are unreliable	Temp. record is unreliable	Antarctica is gaining ice	Environmental Alarmism	New Religion	Conspiracy theorist	Climate's changed before	It's cooling	It's not bad	Technofix (Prometheanism)	Not worth fixing	Leave it to the Market	Anti-libertarian
						Contrarianism				Cornucopianism				Economic Rationalism	
Others															
Sonja Boehmer-Christiansen		X						X							
Philip Foster		X	X	X		X		X							
Lord Monckton		X			X					X	X		X	X	
Benny Peiser		X				X							X		
Bruno Prior													X		X
Stephen Wilde	X					X									
Sub-totals	1	4	1	1	1	4		2		1	1		4	1	1
	17%	67%	17%	17%	17%	67%		33%		17%	17%		67%	17%	17%
All groups combined															
Grand Totals	8	21	6	6	2	12	14	16	8	7	5	5	20	11	9
Percentages	17%	44%	13%	13%	4%	25%	29%	33%	17%	15%	10%	10%	42%	23%	19%

In the following statistical summary, it must be borne in mind that any individual organisation or person may adopt more than one line of argument and/or use more than one rhetorical device. On this basis, it may be seen that, of those whose discourse has been analysed herein, the following may be significant:

- 71% of the (7) sceptical organisations examined claim there is no (legitimate) scientific consensus; whereas 57% believe market-based solutions will solve the problem (if we have one); and 43% believe it is not worth wrecking the economy to fix the problem.
- 71% of the (7) sceptical scientists examined characterise environmentalism as a new "religion"; whereas 57% claim that climate change is being caused by the sun; and 57% also believe that action to tackle ACD is part of a politically motivated (anti-libertarian) conspiracy.
- Similarly, 56% of the (9) sceptical economists examined characterise environmentalism as a new "religion"; whereas 44% believe that action to tackle ACD is part of a financially-motivated scientific conspiracy; and 44% believe it is not worth wrecking the economy to fix the problem.
- 71% of the (7) sceptical journalists or authors examined believe that action to tackle ACD is part of a financially-motivated scientific conspiracy; whereas 57% believe it to be a politically-motivated (anti-libertarian) conspiracy; and characterise concern for the environmental as "alarmism".
- 50% of the (12) sceptical (Conservative) politicians examined claim there is no (legitimate) scientific consensus; and 50% believe it is not worth wrecking the economy to fix the problem, whereas 25% believe those sceptics who claim that ACD stopped in 1998.
- Of the other (6) people examined, two-thirds of them claim there is no (legitimate) scientific consensus; and/or characterise concern for the environment as "alarmism", and/or consider it is not worth wrecking the economy to fix the problem.

Therefore, given the above analysis (as summarised in Table 14), it is now possible to place the six groups (based on the majority position in each case) into the typology of scepticism (proposed in Table 1), as shown in Table 15, below:

Table 15: Majority Classification of Climate Change Sceptics

	Laissez-faire	Reformist
Prosaic	Contrarians **Organisations, Politicians *et al.* (No Consensus) Economists and Scientists (New Religion) Journalists (Conspiracy theorists)**	Economic Rationalists **Politicians and Others** *(It is not worth wrecking the economy to fix the problem)*
Imaginative	Cornucopians (climate change is not significant)	Top-up Views: Prometheans (climate change is not problematic)

With regard to minority views:

- Cornucopian arguments were put forward by only 14% of organisations and/or scientists; 22% of economists; 43% of journalists; 25% of politicians; and 17% of the others.
- Promethean arguments were put forward by only 14% of organisations, none of the scientists; 11% of economists; 29% of journalists; 8% of politicians; and none of the others.

Overall, the most often-cited arguments are:

- that there is no consensus (44%—i.e. 21 out of 48); and
- that it is not worth wrecking the economy to fix the problem (42%—i.e. 20 out of 48).

Conclusions

Whereas the majority of CTTs analysed dispute the existence of a legitimate consensus—and the majority of sceptical journalists focus on conspiracy theories of various kinds—the majority of sceptical scientists and economists equate environmentalism with a new religion. In contrast to all of the above, the politicians and others analysed appear equally likely to cite contrarian and/or economic rationalist arguments.

Climate change sceptics often object to being called "deniers" on the grounds that they accept the climate is changing but do not accept that we are causing it. However, this appeal to reason is wholly reliant on the complexity of climate science; and the consequential limited understanding of it amongst the vast majority of the population.

Therefore, although many sceptical scientists and economists may wish to draw analogies between concern for the environment and religious belief; and may tend to be very dismissive of "an uncritical acceptance of this new conventional wisdom" (Peacock 2008: 114), this does not negate the reality of the *Limits to Growth* argument; nor change the strong probability that, in addition to being the "greatest market failure in history" (Stern) and "a failure of modern politics" (Hamilton), ACD is the clearest evidence yet that the Earth has a limited capacity to cope with the waste products of human activity (cf. Meadows *et al.* 2005: 223). As James Lovelock has put it:

> Unless we see the Earth as a planet that behaves as if it were alive, at least to the extent of regulating its climate and chemistry, we will lack the will to change our way of life and to understand that we have made it our greatest enemy. It is true that many scientists, especially climatologists, now see that our planet has the capacity to regulate its climate and chemistry, but

> this is still a long way from being conventional wisdom (Lovelock 2006: 21-2).

Furthermore, there is strong circumstantial evidence to suggest that this scepticism is being fuelled by those with a vested interest in the continuance of "business as usual" (i.e. the FFL and/or CTTs) by seeking to downplay, deny or dismiss the scientific consensus on the extent of ACD; and/or the unsustainable nature of exponential growth in economic development, resource depletion, and environmental pollution (Hamilton, Jacques, MacKay, Oreskes & Conway, *etc.*). Therefore, unless the vast majority of relevantly-qualified and active climate researchers are mistaken, taking action to mitigate and/or adapt to the realities of ACD in a timely fashion has already been delayed by several decades. This would make it imperative that this delay should end—and that action should be taken.

Given all of the above, climate change scepticism appears to be, in essence, the ideologically-motivated rejection of science: a position that can only be maintained by the rejection of the vast majority of research-based and observable evidence; and/or the invocation of a scientific conspiracy (e.g. to foist environmental alarmism upon a credulous World simply to perpetuate research funding). As such, it is both unwarranted and unsustainable (intellectually or environmentally).

However, because of the economic and political realities of the world in which we live, politicians will not take any action that will be unpopular with business interests and/or the wider electorate. If so, it is also imperative that those with a vested interest in the continuance of "business as usual"—waging this disinformation campaign—should be recognised as not acting in the long-term interests of the global ecosystem and, therefore, human civilisation.

It is hoped that this book will be of benefit to those seeking to achieve this end.

Bibliography

Aaronovitch, D (2010), *Voodoo Histories: How conspiracy theory has shaped modern history.* London: Vintage.

Adam Smith Institute (ASI) (2010), 'Tim Worstall's Chasing Rainbows' [online], *ASI*. Available at <http://www.adamsmith.org/blog/misc/tim-worstall's-chasing-rainbows/> [accessed 13/06/2011].

Adam Smith Institute (ASI) (2011), 'About' [online], *ASI*. Available at <http://www.adamsmith.org/introducing-the-adam-smith-institute/> [accessed 01/06/2011].

Adam (2006), 'Royal Society tells Exxon: stop funding climate change denial' [online] Guardian. Available at <http://www.guardian.co.uk/environment/2006/sep/20/oilandpetrol.business> [accessed 21/07/2011].

Adam, D. (2010), 'Climate emails inquiry: Energy consultant linked to physics body's submission' [online], *Guardian* (5 March 2010). Available at <http://www.guardian.co.uk/environment/2010/mar/05/climate-emails-institute-of-physics-submission> [accessed 27/05/2011].

Appleyard, B. (2011), 'A very heated debate' [online], *Sunday Times* (6 March 2011). Available at <http://repealtheact.co.uk/2011/03/10/a-very-heated-debate/> [accessed 04/06/2011].

Associate Parliamentary Health Group (APHG) (2011), 'Graham Stringer MP' [online], *Associate Parliamentary Health Group*. Available at <http://www.healthinparliament.org.uk/people/graham-stringer-mp> [accessed 14/07/2011].

Barrett, J. & Bellamy, D (2007), 'Climate stability: an inconvenient proof', in *Proceedings of the ICE—Civil Engineering*, 160(2), pp.66-72.

Bate, R. & Morris, J. (1994), *Global Warming: Apocalypse or Hot Air.* London: IEA.

BBC News (2008a), 'New environment boss "sceptical"' [online], *BBC*. Available at <http://news.bbc.co.uk/1/hi/northern_ireland/7446829.stm> [accessed 05/06/2011].

BBC News (2008b), 'Wilson row over green "alarmists"' [online], *BBC*. Available at <http://news.bbc.co.uk/1/hi/northern_ireland/7599810.stm> [accessed 05/06/2011].

Becker, E. (1973), *The Denial of Death*. New York NY: Free Press.

Beckett, A. (2003), 'The changing face of Melanie Phillips' [online], *Guardian* (7 March 2003). Available at <http://www.guardian.co.uk/media/2003/mar/07/dailymail.pressandpublishing/print> [accessed 13/06/2011].

Belfast Telegraph (2008), 'Sammy Wilson: I still think man-made climate change is a con' [online], *Belfast Telegraph* (31 December 2008). Available at <http://www.belfasttelegraph.co.uk/news/environment/environment-minister-sammy-wilson-i-still-think-manmade-climate-change-is-a-con-14123972.html> [accessed 05/06/2011].

Berners-Lee, M. (2010), *How Bad Are Bananas? The Carbon Footprint of Everything*. London: Profile Books.

Biello, (2007), 'Conservative Climate: consensus document may understate the climate change problem' [online], *Scientific American*. Available at <http://www.scientificamerican.com/article.cfm?id=conservative-climate> [accessed 24/05/2011].

Boehmer-Christiansen, S. & Kellow, A. (2002), *International Environmental Policy: Interests and the Failure of the Kyoto Process*. Cheltenham: Edward Elgar.

Boehmer-Christiansen, S. 'What inspired you?' [online], *Spiked*. Available at <http://www.spiked-online.com/index.php?/inspired/article/1341> [accessed 25/05/2011].

Booker, C. (2009), *The Real Global Warming Disaster: Is the Obsession with 'climate Change' Turning Out to be the Most Costly Scientific Blunder in History?* London: Continuum International.

Booker, C. (2010a), 'The climate change scare is dying, but do our MPs notice?' [online], *Daily Telegraph* (13 November 2010). Available at <http://www.telegraph.co.uk/comment/columnists/christopherbooker/8131383/The-climate-change-scare-is-dying-but-do-our-MPs-notice.html> [accessed 10/06/2011].

Booker, C. (2010b), 'Cancun climate conference: the warmists' last Mexican wave' [online], *Daily Telegraph* (4 December 2010). Available at <http://www.telegraph.co.uk/comment/columnists/christopherbooker/8181558/Cancun-climate-conference-the-warmists-last-Mexican-wave.html> [accessed 10/06/2011].

Booker, C. (2011), 'Unscientific hype about the flooding risks from climate change will cost us all dear' [online], *Daily Telegraph* (26 February 2011). Available at <http://www.telegraph.co.uk/comment/columnists/christopherbooker/8349545/Unscientific-hype-about-the-flooding-risks-from-climate-change-will-cost-us-all-dear.html> [accessed 10/06/2011].

Borenstein, S. (2007), 'Data Show "Arctic Is Screaming", Scientists Say' [online], *New York Sun* (12 December 2007). Available at <http://www.nysun.com/foreign/data-show-arctic-is-screaming-scientists-say/> [accessed 26/05/2011].

Bull, P. (2007), 'Political language and persuasive communication', in Weatherall, A. *et al.* (eds) *Language, Discourse and Social Psychology*. Basingstoke: Palgrave Macmillan.

Byatt, I. (2008), 'Weighing the present against the future: the choice, and use, of rates of discount in the analysis of climate change', in Robinson C. (ed), *Climate Change Policy: Challenging the Activists*. London: IEA, pp.92-113.

Carter, N. (2007), *The Politics of the Environment* (2nd ed). Cambridge: Cambridge University Press.

Centre for Policy Studies (2011), 'CPS philosophy' [online], *CPS*. Available at <http://cps.org.uk/index.php?option=com_content&view=cpsarticle&id=36&Itemid=18> [accessed 01/06/2011].

Clacton Gazette (2009), 'Clacton MP in 'climate change' row' [online], *Clacton Gazette* (23 October 2009). Available at <http://www.clactonandfrintongazette.co.uk/news/4699831.Clacton_MP_in_climate_change_row/> [accessed 04/10/2009].

Connor, S. (2010), 'Climate change scandal: MPs exonerate professor' [online], *Independent* (31 March 2010).

Available at <http://www.independent.co.uk/environment/climate-change/climate-change-scandal-mps-exonerate-professor-1931631.html> [accessed 27/05/2011].

Corbyn, P. (2008), 'Global Warming Debate' [online], *WeatherAction*. Available at <http://www.weatheraction.com/pages/pv.asp?p=wact10&fsize=0> [accessed 26/05/2011].

Corbyn, P. (2011a), 'Expect more earthquakes world-wide for next two years' [online], *WeatherAction*. Available at <http://www.weatheraction.com/displayarticle.asp?a=314&c=5> [accessed 26/05/2011].

Corbyn, P. (2011b), 'Piers says it like it is on Australian Radio' [online], *WeatherAction*. Available at <http://www.weatheraction.com/displayarticle.asp?a=324&c=5> [accessed 26/05/2011].

Corbyn, P. (2011c), 'Piers challenges CO2-Warmist "Religion" to come up with evidence at "Climate Week" meeting held in Imperial College' [online], *WeatherAction*. Available at <http://www.weatheraction.com/displayarticle.asp?a=329&c=5> [accessed 26/05/2011].

Courtney, R. (2010), Written evidence to the Science and Technology Select Committee [online], *Crown Copyright*. Available at <http://www.publications.parliament.uk/pa/cm200910/cmselect/cmsctech/memo/climatedata/uc0102.htm> [accessed 26/05/2011].

Daly, H. (1974), 'Steady-state economics versus growthmania: A critique of the orthodox conceptions of growth, wants, scarcity, and efficiency', *Policy Sciences*, 5(2), pp.149-67.

Daly, H. (1992), *Steady State Economics* (2nd ed). London: Earthscan.

Davis, D. (2009), 'Why this ferocious desire to impose hair-shirt policies?' [online], *Independent* (2 December 2009). Available at <http://www.independent.co.uk/opinion/commentators/david-davis-why-this-ferocious-desire-to-impose-hairshirt-policies-1832213.html> [accessed 03/06/2011].

Delingpole, J. (2009), 'Climategate: the final nail in the coffin of Anthropogenic Global Warming?' [online], *Daily Telegraph* (20 November 2009). Available at <http://blogs.telegraph.

co.uk/news/jamesdelingpole/100017393/climategate-the-final-nail-in-the-coffin-of-anthropogenic-global-warming/> [accessed 10/06/2011].

Delingpole, J. (2010), 'Never mind the Climategate whitewash—what about our new £50 billion annual climate bill?' [online], *Daily Telegraph* (7 July 2010). Available at <http://blogs.telegraph.co.uk/news/jamesdelingpole/100046507/never-mind-the-climategate-whitewash-what-about-our-new-50-billion-annual-climate-bill/> [accessed 10/06/2011].

Delingpole, J. (2011), [as interviewed in] 'Horizon: Meet the Climate Sceptics' [online], *BBC* (24 January 2011). Available at <http://www.youtube.com/watch?v=36Xu3SQclE0> [accessed 10/06/2011].

Dept for Transport (2011), 'Public attitudes towards climate change and the impact of transport' [online], *Dept for Transport*. Available at <http://www.dft.gov.uk/adobepdf/162469/221412/221513/4387741/climatechange2011.pdf> [accessed 21/04/2011].

De-Smog Blog, 'About the Climate Cover-up' [online], *De-Smog Blog*. Available at <http://www.desmogblog.com/about-climate-cover> [accessed 02/06/2011].

De-Smog Blog, 'Alister McFarquhar' [online], *De-Smog Blog*. Available at <http://www.desmogblog.com/alister-mcfarquhar> [accessed 02/06/2011].

De-Smog Blog, 'Benny Peiser' [online], *De-Smog Blog*. Available at <http://www.desmogblog.com/benny_peiser> [accessed 07/06/2011].

De-Smog Blog, 'Christopher Monckton' [online], *De-Smog Blog*. Available at <http://www.desmogblog.com/christopher-monckton> [accessed 02/06/2011].

Dickinson, J. (2009), 'The People Paradox: Self-Esteem Striving, Immortality Ideologies, and Human Response to Climate Change', *Ecology and Society* 14(1): 34. [online]. Available at <http://www.ecologyandsociety.org/vol14/iss1/art34/> [accessed 21/06/2011].

Douglas Carswell's Blog, 2009, 'Are Americans ignorant about climate change?', blog post, 29/09/2009, viewed 04/06/2011 <http://www.talkcarswell.com/default.aspx?date=200909>

Douglas Carswell's Blog, 2009, 'BBC and climate change: are we about to see more balanced reporting?', blog post, 12/10/2009, viewed 04/06/2011 <http://www.talkcarswell.com/show.aspx?id=1061>

Dryzek, J. (2005), *The Politics of the Environment* (2nd ed). Oxford: Oxford University Press.

Dyson, F (2008), 'The question of global warming' [online], *The New York Review of Books* [online]. Available at <http://www.nybooks.com/articles/archives/2008/jun/12/the-question-of-global-warming/> [accessed 07/06/2011].

Dyson, T. (2005), 'On Development, Demography and Climate Change: The End of the World as We Know It?', *Population and Environment* 27(2), pp.117-149.

Ehrlich, P. & Ehrlich, A. (1996), *Betrayal of Science and Reason: How Anti-Environmental Rhetoric Threatens Our Future*. Washington, DC: Island Press.

Elster, J. (1986), *An Introduction to Karl Marx*. Cambridge: Cambridge University Press.

Energy and Environment Journal, *Mission Statement* [online], *MultiScience*. Available at <http://www.multi-science.co.uk/ee-mission.htm> [accessed 26/05/2011].

Environment Agency (EA) (2011), 'Pollution Inventory substances A-C: Carbon Dioxide' [online], *EA*. Available at <http://www.environment-agency.gov.uk/business/topics/pollution/31.aspx> [accessed 25/05/2011].

Fairclough, N. (2003), *Analysing Discourse*. London: Routledge

Festinger, L. (1957), *The Theory of Cognitive Dissonance*. Stanford CA: Stanford University Press.

Foster, P. (2010), *While Earth Endures: Creation, Cosmology and Climate Change* (2nd ed). Huntingdon: St Matthew Publishing Ltd.

Gascoigne, N. (2002), *Scepticism*. Chesham: Acumen.

Gavin, N. & Marshall, T. (2011), 'Mediated climate change in Britain: Scepticism on the web and on television around Copenhagen' [online], *Global Environmental Change*.

Available at <http://www.sciencedirect.com/science/article/pii/S0959378011000343> [accessed 21/06/2011].

Gore, A. (2005), *Transcript of Speech to Sierra Club National Convention*, 09/05/2005 [online]. Available at <http://www.commondreams.org/views05/0912-32.htm> [accessed 21/04/2011].

Gray, L. (2010), 'Climate sceptics launch campaign to overturn green targets' [online], *Daily Telegraph* (27 October 2010). Available at <http://www.telegraph.co.uk/earth/environment/climatechange/8088204/Climate-sceptics-launch-campaign-to-overturn-green-targets.html> [accessed 06/08/2011].

Greenpeace, (2010), 'Exposing the dirty money behind fake climate science' [online], *Greenpeace International*. Available at <http://www.greenpeace.org/international/en/news/features/dirty-money-climate-30032010/> [accessed 27/05/2011].

Grice, A. (2009), 'Cameron hit by Tory backlash on environment' [online], *Independent* (2 December 2009). Available at <http://www.independent.co.uk/news/uk/politics/cameron-hit-by-tory-backlash-on-environment-1832208.html> [accessed 03/06/2011].

GWPF (2009), 'History and Mission' [online], *GWPF*. Available at <http://www.thegwpf.org/who-we-are/history-and-mission.html> [accessed 01/06/2011].

Hamilton, C. (2010a), *Requiem for a Species: Why we resist the truth about climate change.* London: Earthscan.

Hamilton, C. (2010b), 'Climate denial versus climate science' [online]. Available at <http://www.clivehamilton.net.au/cms/media/documents/speeches/launch_speech_for_website.pdf> [accessed 20/07/2011].

Hannan, D. (2009), 'Climate change: the case for scepticism', blog post, 02/12/2009, viewed 04/06/2011 <http://blogs.telegraph.co.uk/news/danielhannan/100018669/climate-change-the-case-for-scepticism/>.

Hansard (2005), House of Commons Debates Volume 430(36) [online]. Available at <http://www.publications.parliament.uk/pa/cm200405/cmhansrd/vo050208/debtext/50208-07.htm#50208-07_spnew10> [accessed 11/07/2011].

Hansard (2007), House of Commons Debates Volume 461(106) [online]. Available at <http://www.publications.parliament.uk/pa/cm200607/cmhansrd/cm070615/debtext/70615-0009.htm> [accessed 04/06/2011].

Hansard (2008a), House of Commons Debates Volume 477(106) [online]. Available at <http://www.publications.parliament.uk/pa/cm200708/cmhansrd/cm080609/debtext/80609-0016.htm> [accessed 04/06/2011].

Hansard (2008b), House of Commons Debates Volume 481(153) [online]. Available at <http://www.publications.parliament.uk/pa/cm200708/cmhansrd/cm081028/debtext/81028-0010.htm> [accessed 04/06/2011].

Hansard (2008c), House of Commons Debates Volume 481(153) [online]. Available at <http://www.publications.parliament.uk/pa/cm200708/cmhansrd/cm081028/debtext/81028-0021.htm> [accessed 04/06/2011].

Hansard (2009), House of Commons Debates Volume 492(76) [online]. Available at http://www.publications.parliament.uk/pa/cm200809/cmhansrd/cm090514/debtext/90514-0005.htm [accessed 04/06/2011].

Heartland Institute (2008), 'Manhattan Declaration on Climate Change' [online]. Available at <http://www.heartland.org/policybot/results/22866/New_York_Global_Warming_Conference_Considers_Manhattan_Declaration.html> [accessed 27/05/2011].

Helmer, R. (2009), Speech in European Parliament on 4 February 2009 [online]. Available at <http://www.europarl.europa.eu/sides/getDoc.do?pubRef=-//EP//TEXT+CRE+20090204+ITEM-003+DOC+XML+V0//EN&language=EN&query=INTERV&detail=3-019> [accessed 04/06/2011].

Henderson, D. (2008), 'Governments and climate change issues: questioning the consensus', in Robinson C. (ed), *Climate Change Policy: Challenging the Activists*. London: IEA, pp.70-91.

Henson R., (2008), *The Rough Guide to Climate Change* (2nd Ed). London: Rough Guides.

Independent Minds (2010), 'Chasing Rainbows by Tim Worstall' [online], *Stacey International*. Available at <http://www.stacey-international.co.uk/v1/site/product_rpt.asp?Catid=365&catname=> [accessed 15/07/2011].

Independent, The (2010), *Climate change science is vindicated* [online]. *Independent* (8 July 2010). Available at <http://www.independent.co.uk/opinion/leading-articles/leading-article-climate-change-science-is-vindicated-2020929.html> [accessed 27/04/2011].

Inhofe, J. (2003), *Transcript of Speech in US Senate*, 28/07/2003 [online]. Available at <http://inhofe.senate.gov/pressreleases/climate.htm> [accessed 21/04/2011].

Institute of Economic Affairs (IEA), 'About us' [online], *IEA*. Available at <http://www.iea.org.uk/about> [accessed 25/05/2011].

Institute of Economic Affairs (IEA), 'What we do' [online], *IEA*. Available at <http://www.iea.org.uk/about/what-we-do> [accessed 25/05/2011].

IPN (2006), 'IPN response to the Royal Society and The Guardian's accusations on IPN's work on Climate Change' [online] *IPN*. Available at <http://www.policynetwork.net/environment/media/ipn-response-royal-society-and-guardians-accusations-ipns-work-climate-change> [accessed 21/07/2011].

International Policy Network (IPN) (2010), 'Julian Morris' [online], *IPN*. Available at <http://www.policynetwork.net/individual/julian-morris> [accessed 14/07/2011].

Jacques, P. et al. (2008), 'The organisation of denial: Conservative think tanks and environmental scepticism', *Environmental Politics*, 17(3), pp.349-385.

Jacques, P. (2009), *Environmental Skepticism: Ecology, Power and Public Life*. Farnham: Ashgate.

Lawson, N. (2008), *An Appeal to Reason: A cool look at global warming*. London: Duckworth Overlook.

Lawson, N. (2009), *An Appeal to Reason: A cool look at global warming* [online], Amazon. Available at <http://www.amazon.co.uk/Appeal-Reason-Cool-Global-Warming/dp/0715638416/

ref=cm_cr_pr_product_top#reader_0715638416> [accessed 25/05/2011].

Le Page, M (2007), 'Climate myths: Many leading scientists question climate change' [online], *New Scientist*. Available at <http://www.newscientist.com/article/dn11654-climate-myths-many-leading-scientists-question-climate-change.html> [accessed 21/04/2011].

Lewis, R. (2007), 'Global Warming: False Alarms' [online], *IEA*. Available at <http://www.iea.org.uk/publications/research/global-warming-false-alarms-web-publication> [accessed 09/06/2011].

Lewis, R. (2008), 'Global alarmism', in Robinson C. (ed), *Climate Change Policy: Challenging the Activists*. London: IEA, pp.26-41.

Lilley, P. (2009a), 'Copenhagen Climate Change Conference' (extract from Parliamentary debate) [online]. Available at <http://www.peterlilley.co.uk/article.aspx?id=19&ref=1480> [accessed 03/06/2011].

Lilley, P. (2009b), 'Climate Change: Preparation for the Copenhagen Climate Change Conference' (extract from Parliamentary debate) [online]. Available at <http://www.peterlilley.co.uk/article.aspx?id=19&ref=1504> [accessed 03/06/2011].

Lilley, P. (2010), 'About Peter' [online]. Available at <http://www.peterlilley.co.uk/text.aspx?id=2> [accessed 03/06/2011].

Live Science (2010), 'Majority of Americans still believe in Global Warming' [online], *Live Science*. Available at <http://www.livescience.com/6567-majority-americans-global-warming.html> [accessed 21/04/2011].

Liverpool James Moore University (LJMU) (2011), 'Dr Benny Peiser' [online], *LJMU*. Available at <http://www.staff.livjm.ac.uk/spsbpeis/> [accessed 07/06/2011].

Lomborg, B. (2010), *Smart Solutions to Climate Change: Comparing Costs and Benefits*. Cambridge: Cambridge University Press.

Lovelock, J. (2006), *Revenge of Gaia*. London: Allen Lane.

Luke, T. (2000), 'A rough road out of Rio: The right-wing reaction against global

Environmentalism', in Low, N. *et al.* (eds.) *Consuming cities: The urban environment in the global economy after the Rio declaration.* New York: Routledge, pp.54-69.

MacKay, D. (2009), *Sustainable Energy: without the Hot Air.* Cambridge: UIT. Available online at <http://withouthotair.com> [accessed 21/04/2010].

McDonald, H. & Jowit, J. (2009) 'DUP stands by climate change sceptic environment minister' [online], *Guardian* (10 February 2009). Available at <http://www.guardian.co.uk/environment/2009/feb/10/sammy-wilson-climate-change?intcmp=239> [accessed 05/06/2011].

Meadows D., *et al.* (2005), *Limits to Growth: the 30-Year Update.* London: Earthscan.

Monbiot, G (1997), 'The Revolution has been televised' [online], *Guardian* (18 December 1997). Available at <http://www.monbiot.com/1997/12/18/the-revolution-has-been-televised/> [accessed 13/06/2011].

Monbiot, G. (2005), 'Junk Science' [online] *Guardian*. Available at <http://www.monbiot.com/2005/05/10/junk-science/> [accessed 15/06/2011].

Monbiot, G. (2009), 'Monbiot's royal flush: Top 10 climate change deniers' [online], *Guardian*. Available at <http://www.guardian.co.uk/environment/georgemonbiot/2009/mar/06/climate-change-deniers-top-10> [accessed 21/04/2011].

Monbiot, G. (2011), 'About George' [online], *Monbiot.com*. Available at <http://www.monbiot.com/about/> [accessed 21/04/2011].

Monckton, C. (2010), 'Unsound Advice' [online], *SPPI*. Available at <http://scienceandpublicpolicy.org/monckton/unsound_advice.html> [accessed 06/06/2011].

Montford, A. (2010a), *The Hockey Stick Illusion.* London: Stacey International.

Montford, A. (2010b) 'The Climategate Inquiries' [online], *GWPF* (14 September 2010). Available at <http://www.thegwpf.org/gwpf-reports/1531-the-climategate-inquries.html> [accessed 10/06/2011].

Morris, J. (2008), 'Which policy to address climate change', in Robinson C. (ed), *Climate Change Policy: Challenging the Activists*. London: IEA, pp.132-58.

Moselle, B. & Moore, S. (2011), 'Climate Change Policy—Time for Plan B' [online], *Policy Exchange*. Available at <http://www.policyexchange.org.uk/images/publications/pdfs/Climate_Change_Policy_-_Time_for_Plan_B.pdf>[accessed 21/07/2011].

Naess, A. (1968), *Scepticism*. London: Routledge & Kegan Paul.

Newell, P. (2000), *Climate for Change: Non-State Actors and the Global Politics of the Greenhouse*, Cambridge: Cambridge University Press.

O'Neill, B. (2006), 'Global warming: the chilling effect on free speech' [online], *Spiked* (6 October 2006). Available at <http://www.spiked-online.com/index.php?/site/article/1782/> [accessed 13/06/2011].

O'Neill, B. (2011a), 'The icy grip of the politics of fear' [online], *Spiked* (4 January 2011). Available at <http://www.spiked-online.com/index.php/site/article/10046/> [accessed 14/06/2011].

O'Neill, B. (2011b), 'The persecution of Johnny Ball and how gross intolerance is crushing free debate on climate change' [online], *Telegraph*. Available at <http://blogs.telegraph.co.uk/news/brendanoneill2/100076870/the-persecution-of-johnny-ball-and-how-gross-intolerance-is-crushing-free-debate-on-climate-change/> [accessed 14/06/2011].

Oakeshott, M. (1996), *The Politics of Faith and the Politics of Scepticism*. New Haven CT: Yale University Press.

Ofcom (1998), 'Complaints & Interventions Report for Against Nature' [online], *Ofcom*. Available at <http://www.ofcom.org.uk/static/archive/itc/itc_publications/complaints_reports/programme_complaints/show_complaint.asp-prog_complaint_id=40.html> [accessed 13/06/2011].

Ofcom (2007), 'Broadcast Bulletin Issue number 114—21/07/08' [online], *Ofcom*. Available at <http://stakeholders.ofcom.org.uk/enforcement/broadcast-bulletins/obb114/> [accessed 13/06/2100].

Oreskes, N. & Conway E. (2010), *Merchants of Doubt*. New York, NY: Bloomsbury Press.

Orlowski, A. (2010), 'Parliament misled over Climategate report, says MP' [online], *GWPF*. Available at <http://www.thegwpf.org/science-news/1220-parliament-misled-over-climategate-report-says-mp.html> [accessed 28/05/2011]

Peacock, A. (2008), 'Climate change, religion and human freedom', in Robinson C. (ed), *Climate Change Policy: Challenging the Activists*. London: IEA, pp.114-31.

Peiser, B. (2011), 'Climate fatigue leaves global warming in the cold' [online], *Public Service*. Available at <http://www.publicserviceeurope.com/article/136/climate-fatigue-leaves-global-warming-in-the-cold> [accessed 07/06/2011].

Philips, M. (2002a), 'The global warming con-trick' [online], *Daily Mail* (25 February 2002). Available at <http://www.melaniephillips.com/the-global-warming-con-trick> [accessed 13/06/2011].

Philips, M. (2002b), 'Wet, but not the end of the world' [online], *Daily Mail* (12 August 2002). Available at <http://www.melaniephillips.com/wet-but-not-the-end-of-the-world> [accessed 13/06/2011].

Philips, M. (2004), 'The global warming fraud' [online], *Daily Mail* (12 January 2004). Available at <http://www.melaniephillips.com/the-global-warming-fraud> [accessed 13/06/2011].

Philips, M. (2008), 'Our political landscape' [online], *The Spectator* (28 September 2008). Available at <http://www.spectator.co.uk/melaniephillips/2182141/our-political-landscape.thtml> [accessed 13/06/2011].

Philips, M. (2009), 'The deep green fear of the human race' [online], *Daily Mail* (2 February 2009). Available at <http://www.melaniephillips.com/the-dep-green-fear-of-the-human-race> [accessed 13/06/2011].

Phillips, M. (2010), 'Biography' [online], *MelaniePhillips.com*. Available at <http://www.melaniephillips.com/biography> [accessed 13/06/2011].

Pirie, M. (2009), 'Lord Stern is wrong: giving up meat is no way to save the planet' [online], *ASI*. Available at <http://www.adamsmith.org/think-piece/environment/lord-stern-is-

wrong%3a-giving-up-meat-is-no-way-to-save-the-planet/> [accessed 01/06/2011].

Prior, B. (2008), 'Foreword,' in Robinson C. (ed), *Climate Change Policy: Challenging the Activists*. London: IEA, pp.11-15.

Redwood, J. (2006), 'About John Redwood' [online]. Available at <http://www.johnredwoodsdiary.com/about-john-redwood/> [accessed 03/06/2011].

Redwood, J. (2007), 'The global warming "swindle"' [online]. Available at <http://www.johnredwoodsdiary.com/2007/03/09/the-global-warming-swindle/> [accessed 03/06/2011].

Redwood, J. (2010), 'Those climate projections in full' [online]. Available at <http://www.johnredwoodsdiary.com/2010/01/27/those-climate-change-projections-in-full/> [accessed 03/06/2011].

Robinson, C. (2008a), 'Climate change and the market economy: introduction', in Robinson C. (ed), *Climate Change Policy: Challenging the Activists*. London: IEA, pp.19-25.

Robinson, C. (2008b), 'Climate change, centralised action and markets', in Robinson C. (ed), *Climate Change Policy: Challenging the Activists*. London: IEA, pp.42-69.

Robinson, W. (Peter) (2007), 'False beliefs and unsound arguments promoted by authorities', in Weatherall, A., *et al.* (eds) *Language, Discourse and Social Psychology*. Basingstoke: Palgrave Macmillan.

Russell, M. (2010), *The Independent Climate Change E-mails Review* [online]. Available at <http://www.cce-review.org/> [accessed 25/05/2011].

Scientific Alliance (2010a), 'About the Scientific Alliance' [online], *Scientific Alliance*. Available at <http://www.scientific-alliance.org/home/about-scientific-alliance> [accessed 27/05/2011].

Scientific Alliance (2010b), 'Scientific Advisory Forum' [online], *Scientific Alliance*. Available at <http://www.scientific-alliance.org/scientific-advisory-forum> [accessed 01/06/2011].

SEPP (1995), 'The Leipzig Declaration on Global Climate Change' [online], *SEPP*. Available at <http://sovereignty.net/p/clim/leipzig.htm> [accessed 16/06/2011].

Sinclair, M. (2009), 'Ending the Green Rip-off: Reforming climate change policy to reduce the burden on families' [online], *Taxpayers' Alliance*. Available at <http://www.taxpayersalliance.com/egro.pdf> [accessed 21/07/2011].

Singer, S. Fred (2008), 'Foggy science In London' [online], *Climate Realists*. Available at <http://climaterealists.com/?id=1336> [accessed 01/06/2011].

Skeptical Science (2011), 'What does Naomi Oreskes' study on consensus show?' [online], *Skeptical Science*. Available at <http://www.skepticalscience.com/print.php?r=49> [accessed 07/06/2011].

Smith, G. (2003), *Deliberative Democracy and the Environment*. London: Routledge.

SourceWatch (2009) 'Jack Barrett' [online], *CMD*. Available at <http://www.sourcewatch.org/index.php?title=Jack_Barrett> [accessed 15/06/2011].

SourceWatch (2010) 'SourceWatch: Purpose' [online], *CMD*. Available at <http://www.sourcewatch.org/index.php?title=SourceWatch:About> [accessed 15/06/2011].

SourceWatch (2011), 'David Bellamy' [online], *CMD*. Available at <http://www.sourcewatch.org/index.php?title=David_Bellamy> [accessed 27/05/2011].

Spiked (2011), 'About Spiked' [online], *Spiked*. Available at <http://www.spiked-online.com/index.php/about/article/336/> [accessed 14/06/2011].

SPPI (2010), 'Our Mission' [online], *SPPI*. Available at <http://scienceandpublicpolicy.org/our_mission.html> [accessed 06/06/2011].

Stern, N. (2009), *A Blueprint for a Safer Planet*. London: Bodley Head.

Stern, N., et al. (2006), *Stern Review: The Economics of Climate Change*. London: HM Treasury.

Strangeways, I. (2008), 'Issues in Meteorological Observing Networks', in Minutes of Meeting 6 March 2008 [online], *Royal Meteorological Society*. Available at <http://www.

rmets.org/activities/groups/centres/minutes.php?ID=18> [accessed 31/05/2011].

Strangeways, I. (2009), *Measuring Global Temperatures: Analysis and Interpretation*. Cambridge: Cambridge University Press.

Strangeways, I. (2011), 'The Greenhouse Effect: a closer look', *Weather* 66(2), pp.44-8.

Stubbs, M (1983), Discourse Analysis: The sociolinguistic analysis of natural language. Oxford: Blackwell.

Thacker, P. (2005), 'Skeptics get a journal' [online], *Environmental Science & Technology*. Available at <http://www.realclimate.org/docs/thacker/skeptics.pdf> [accessed 25/05/2011].

WeatherAction (2010), 'News 35—Climate Fools Day 2010' [online], *WeatherAction*. Available at <http://www.weatheraction.com/docs/WANews10No35.pdf> [accessed 28/05/2011].

West Virginia Coal Association (2009) 'Environment minister Sammy Wilson: I still think man-made climate change is a con' [online], *WVCA*. Available at <http://www.wvcoal.com/Latest/environment-minister-sammy-wilson-i-still-think-man-made-climate-change-is-a-con.html> [accessed 05/06/2011].

Wikipedia (2011a), 'Climate change denial' [online], *Wikipedia*. Available at <http://en.wikipedia.org/wiki/Climate_change_denial> [accessed 21/04/2011].

Wikipedia (2011b), 'List of scientists opposing the mainstream scientific assessment of global warming' [online], *Wikipedia*. Available at <http://en.wikipedia.org/wiki/List_of_scientists_opposing_the_mainstream_scientific_assessment_of_global_warming> [accessed 21/04/2011].

Wikipedia (2011c), 'Piers Corbyn' [online], *Wikipedia*. Available at <http://en.wikipedia.org/wiki/Piers_Corbyn> [accessed 26/05/2011].

Wikipedia (2011d), 'Christopher Booker' [online], Wikipedia. Available at <http://en.wikipedia.org/wiki/Christopher_Booker> [accessed 10/06/2011].

Wikipedia (2011e), 'James Delingpole' [online], *Wikipedia*. Available at <http://en.wikipedia.org/wiki/James_Delingpole> [accessed 10/06/2011].

Wikipedia (2011f), 'Andrew Montford' [online], *Wikipedia*. Available at <http://en.wikipedia.org/wiki/Andrew_Montford> [accessed 10/06/2011].

Wikipedia (2011g), Tim Worstall [online], *Wikipedia*. Available at <http://en.wikipedia.org/wiki/Tim_Worstall> [accessed 13/06/2011].

Wikipedia (2011h), 'Christopher Monckton, 3rd Viscount Monckton of Brenchley' [online], *Wikipedia*. Available at <http://en.wikipedia.org/wiki/Christopher_Monckton,_3rd_Viscount_Monckton_of_Brenchley> [accessed 06/06/2011].

Wilde, S. (2008), 'The Death Blow to Anthropogenic Global Warming' [online], *Climate Realists*. Available at <http://climaterealists.com/index.php?id=1396> [accessed 31/05/2011].

Wilde, S. (2011), 'How Gavin Schmidt and Michael Mann almost got it right in 2001' [online], *Climate Realists*. Available at <http://climaterealists.com/index.php?id=7758> [accessed 31/05/2011].

Williams, M. (1991), *Unnatural Doubts*. Blackwell: Oxford.

Wilson, S. (2011a), 'Sammy's Newsletter Column 1 Jan 2011' [online]. Available at <http://www.sammywilson.org/2011/01/04/sammys-newsletter-column-1-jan-2011/> [accessed 05/06/2011].

Wilson, S. (2011b), 'Air passenger duty is damaging local economy' [online]. Available at <http://www.sammywilson.org/2011/04/15/wilson-air-passenger-duty-is-damaging-local-economy/> [accessed 05/06/2011].

Wilson, S. (2011c), 'Issues' [online]. Available at <http://www.sammywilson.org/issues/> [accessed 05/06/2011].

Wilson, S. (2011d), 'Biography' [online]. Available at <http://www.sammywilson.org/biography/> [accessed 06/06/2011].

Wodak, R. (2001), 'What CDA is about—a summary of its history, important concepts and its developments', in Wodak, R. & Meyer, M. (eds), *Methods of Critical Discourse Analysis*. London: Sage.

Worstall, T. (2007), 'About' [online], *Tim Worstall*. Available at <http://timworstall.com/about/> [accessed 13/06/2011].

WWF (2008), 'Climate Change: Faster, Stronger, Sooner' [online], *World Wildlife Fund*. Available at <http://www.wwf.org.uk/wwf_articles.cfm?unewsid=2289> [accessed 27/05/2011].

Appendix—
Supporting Evidence

Organisations

Adam Smith Institute (ASI)

The ASI styles itself as ". . . the UK's leading libertarian think tank"; and says that it ". . . engineers policies to increase Britain's economic competitiveness, inject choice into public services, and create a freer, more prosperous society." ASI (2011)

Pirie's essential argument is summed up in the subheading to his article: "Technological advances, not 'live more simply' environmentalism, will deliver a greener planet" (Pirie 2009). Not only is the logic of Stern's suggestion that we should all become vegetarians (because it is more efficient way of obtaining energy from food) not contested, this is a very straightforward statement of belief in human ingenuity as the means by which the problem of finite resources—if not ACD—may be solved. In other words, this is Prometheanism rather than Cornucopianism (i.e. the means of salvation rests with humanity rather than in nature).

Centre for Policy Studies (CPS)

The CPS was founded by Sir Keith Joseph and Margaret Thatcher in 1974 to promote the principles of a free society and, so it claims, has since played a global role in the dissemination of free market economics (CPS 2011). Its website also proclaims that it:

> ... believes in freedom and responsibility ... develops and promotes policies to limit the role of the state, to encourage enterprise and to enable the institutions of society—such as families and voluntary organizations—to flourish (ibid).

As well as being very reminiscent of our current government's promotion of the idea of a "Big Society", this is clearly a manifesto for market solutions to all problems. Furthermore, amongst the items in its back catalogue are the following:

- *Climate Change: a guide to the scientific uncertainties* (February 2007), in which Martin Livermore "... stresses that, despite claims to the contrary, the scientific understanding of climate change is far from complete"; and
- *Not so simple?* (May 2008), in which a certain Fred Singer (PhD) presents a scientific response to the Royal Society's paper *Climate Change Controversies: a simple guide* (published in 2007).

See also <http://www.publicservice.co.uk/feature_story.asp?id=9867> [accessed 01/06/2011].

With regard to the latter, Singer's own introduction to the pamphlet (as posted on the *Climate Realists* website) is very revealing (Singer 2008). In it, he claims there is no "independent" evidence for ACD (i.e. the IPCC is not independent), which is therefore conspiracy theory on a grand scale. However, for the CPS (and arguably every other right-wing think tank), the most important conclusion is probably that: "Panicky reactions to exaggerated scenarios of global warming are bound to be costly and do great damage to world economic development" (ibid). The only problem with this statement, as Stern (2006) and Clive Hamilton (2010a) have demonstrated, is that it is not true: As Hamilton has pointed out, all that Stern was advocating was shaving 1 or 2% off total economic growth over the next 40 years (Hamilton 2010a: 54). Of course mitigation sounds costly when expressed in terms of trillions of US dollars but, in terms of delayed doubling-time for average salaries it may not be (i.e. 41 years instead of 40).

Global Warming Policy Foundation (GWPF)

Speaking at the launch of the GWPF, Lord Lawson said that it is unique because it is:

> . . . an all-party and non-party think tank . . . which, while open-minded on the contested science of global warming, is deeply concerned about the costs and other implications of many of the policies currently being advocated. We are in no sense 'anti-environmental' . . . . Our concern is solely with the possible effects of any future global warming and the policy responses that [these] may evoke. GWPF (2009)

Institute for Economic Affairs (IEA)

The mission statement of the IEA reads as follows:

> . . . Our mission is to improve understanding of the fundamental institutions of a free society by analysing and expounding the role of markets in solving economic and social problems. Given the current economic challenges facing Britain and the wider global environment, it is more vital than ever that we promote the intellectual case for a free economy, low taxes . . . and lower levels of regulation. The IEA also challenges people to think about the correct role of institutions, property rights and the rule of law in creating a society that fosters innovation, entrepreneurship and the efficient use of environmental resources (IEA—*About us*).

Similarly, under the heading "What we do", the IEA website says:

> The IEA holds no corporate position . . . Nevertheless, all those associated with the Institute support free markets [. . . and . . .] believe that society's problems and challenges are best dealt with by individuals, companies and voluntary associations interacting with each other freely without interference from politicians and the state. This means that government action, whether through taxes, regulation or the legal system, should be kept to a minimum (IEA—*What we do*).

International Policy Network (IPN)

Arguably, the most illuminating part of the IPN's press release reads as follows:

> Notwithstanding that concern, the IPCC is not a scientific body: it is a consensus-oriented political body. An examination of the IPCC process . . . makes it clear that the choice of authors and reviewers as well as the final review of its Reports is conducted by government officials, who may or may not be scientists. In any case, science is inherently antithetical to consensus: science is a process that involves continuously questioning and challenging what we know in order to improve our understanding of the world.
>
> If indeed the IPCC has become politicised by people who see it as part of "the final push that they need to take action," then it is all the more important to encourage debate about what the IPCC says. This is quite different from seeking "to undermine" the IPCC.
>
> From Mr [Bob] Ward's statements, one is led to the conclusion that the Royal Society is seeking to close

down legitimate debate about climate change. This is most depressing and makes one wonder whether the Royal Society, had it existed in the Third Century BC, would have joined with other members of the Athenian elite in opposing Aristarchus of Samos, who had deduced that the Earth revolved around the Sun. Likewise, one wonders whether it would have joined with the Catholic Church in condemning the heretical heliocentric views of Nicolaus Copernicus Galileo Galilei (IPN 2006).

Scientific Alliance (SA)

The SA website indicates that it is a not-for-profit membership-based organisation that:

> ... brings together both scientists and non-scientists committed to rational discussion and debate on the challenges facing the environment today ... concerned about the many ways in which science is often misinterpreted, and at times misrepresented, within both policy circles and in the media ... [and thus work] ... to overcome this misunderstanding by aiming to ... promote sound science in the environmental debate (SA 2010a).

Weather Action (WA)

WA (the brainchild of meteorologist Piers Corbyn) was the main organising force behind *Climate Fools Day* in the Houses of Parliament on 27 October 2010 (to mark the 2nd anniversary of the passage into law of the Climate Change Act 2008). The flyer for this event highlights a supposed necessity for "evidence-based science and policy" rather than the "Carbon Con" [sic]. It goes on to suggest: "If the UK had been relying on wind farms there would have been blackouts all over, freeze-ups, more burst-pipes & cold-weather deaths. This is the madness CO_2-Global Warmist religion is leading Britain towards" (WA 2010).

As such, ACD is clearly presented as a myth; not based on evidence, and pursued by politicians who have been duped by the proponents of a new religion (i.e. outright Contrarianism).

Scientists

Jack Barrett

According to SourceWatch, Jack Barrett is not a climate scientist; and has only ever published a single peer-reviewed paper on the subject of cloud densification (SourceWatch 2009).

Barrett was one of the keynote speakers at a conference in Leipzig in November 1995 organized by the European Academy for Environmental Affairs and the Science and Environmental Policy Project (SEPP),[a] at which he is on record has having said that if atmospheric concentration of CO2 were to double, it would only result in minimal temperature rise (<1°C) that ". . . cannot justify the commotion about global warming" (ibid). Furthermore, the conference resulted in the Leipzig Declaration on Global Climate Change, which included the assertion that, ". . . there does not exist today a general scientific consensus about the importance of greenhouse warming from rising levels of carbon dioxide" (SEPP 1995).

He is on the Advisory Forum of the Scientific Alliance, whose website confirms his area of expertise as being chemistry: "[Dr Barrett] is the author of several textbooks about inorganic chemistry and the bacterial oxidation of minerals and is especially interested in the science of climate change" (SA 2010b).

David Bellamy

In 2007, Barrett co-authored a paper with botanist David Bellamy entitled 'Climate stability: an inconvenient proof', published in the Institute of Civil Engineer's *Civil Engineering* journal, the abstract of which reads:

> This paper demonstrates that the widely prophesied doubling of atmospheric carbon dioxide levels from natural, pre-industrial values will enhance the so-called 'greenhouse effect' but will amount to less than 1°C of global warming. It also points out that such a scenario is unlikely to arise given our limited reserves of fossil fuels—certainly not before the end of this century. Furthermore, the paper argues that general circulation models are as yet insufficiently accurate for civil engineers to rely on their predictions in any forward-planning decisions—the omission of solar wind effects being a potentially significant shortcoming . . . (Barrett & Bellamy 2007: 66).

The use of terms such as 'widely-prophesied', and 'so-called' indicate the authors' scepticism regarding CO_2 being the primary cause of any ongoing climate change (i.e. Contrarianism as defined herein). Reference to the finite nature of fossil fuel reserves seems somewhat weak and a little premature (although just because they are there does not mean we should dig them up). The strongest argument appears to be that against the uncertainty in modelling. However, as Hamilton has recently pointed out, the wide range of results reported by the probabilistic models now in use, ". . . is not due to uncertainties about how much warming is associated with a given concentration of greenhouse gases . . . but to the difficulty in forecasting the . . . world's greenhouse gas emissions" (Hamilton 2010a: 6). Therefore, Barrett and Bellamy's paper, published in an inappropriate medium appears to be relying on the ignorance of the reader in order to gain some credence for its sceptical message.

On 16 April 2005, David Bellamy had a letter published in the *New Scientist* magazine, in which he claimed (amongst other things) that "555 of all the 625 glaciers under observation by the World Glacier Monitoring Service [WGMS] in Zurich, Switzerland, have been growing since 1980" (cited in Monbiot 2005). However, upon investigation, George Monbiot discovered that this was a typing error (it should have been "55%") but, even then, this was disavowed by the WGMS. When Monbiot investigated further, he discovered that SEPP was the original source of the 55% claim and, when questioned, Singer cited "a paper published in Science in 1989." However, after exhaustive research Monbiot could find no such paper (ibid). Be that as it may, none of this has prevented Bellamy's claims from being erroneously circulated on the Internet as well.

According to SourceWatch, despite being a botanist by vocation, David Bellamy was an invited speaker at the Scientific Alliance's 2005 'Apocalypse No—Assessing Catastrophic Climate Change' conference in London, and the Heartland Institute's 2008 'International Conference on Climate Change' in New York. (SourceWatch 2011)

The latter was also the birthplace of the so-called *Manhattan Declaration on Climate Change*, part of which reads as follows:

> That current plans to restrict anthropogenic CO_2 emissions are a dangerous misallocation of intellectual capital and resources that should be dedicated to solving humanity's real and serious problems. That there is no convincing evidence that CO_2 emissions from modern industrial activity has in the past, is now, or will in the future cause catastrophic climate change. That attempts by governments to inflict taxes and costly regulations on industry and individual citizens with the aim of reducing emissions of CO_2 will pointlessly curtail the prosperity of the West and progress of developing nations without affecting climate. That adaptation as needed is massively more

cost-effective than any attempted mitigation and that a focus on such mitigation will divert the attention and resources of governments away from addressing the real problems of their peoples. That human-caused climate change is not a global crisis (Heartland Institute 2008).

If this may be taken as a proxy for Bellamy's views, which seems a reasonable assumption, then he (and everyone who attended the conference and signed the declaration), would appear to endorse Henson's *Rough Guide to Climate Change* caricature of Contrarianism in each and every aspect.

Piers Corbyn

The *Weather Action* website includes a section on the *Global Warming Debate*, which is actually Piers Corbyn's personal response to BBC TV's *Climate Wars* mini-series presented by (earth scientist) Professor Iain Stewart in 2008. In this response, Corbyn describes the programme (first broadcast on 14/09/2008) as ". . . a shameful and desperate effort from the BBC's 'green religion department' to shore up the failing theory of CO_2-driven global warming . . . which puts lipstick on scientific fraud but it remains fraud" (Corbyn 2008).

Moving on to the so-called hockey stick graph of temperature reconstructions using proxy data (featured in the programme), Corbyn criticises this in similar fashion and, somewhat remarkably for a widely-acclaimed physicist and astrophysicist, he appears happy to "concur fully" with the facts presented—and conclusions reached—by the non-scientist Lord Monckton (ibid). Next, Corbyn asserts that global warming stopped in 1998 (another claim commonly found in cyberspace) because world "temperatures have been generally declining for about 10 years while CO_2 is rising rapidly" (ibid). He then concludes his critique by claiming that Greenland was so-named by the Vikings because it was covered in less ice 1000 years ago than it is today, and accuses the IPCC of "deliberately ignoring or covering-up these facts . . ." (ibid). Although this response to Climate Wars was an initial response, it does not appear to have been amended since. Furthermore, although full of rhetoric, it includes no reference to peer-reviewed scientific data to back-up the claims made and/or "facts" stated. For such an eminently qualified scientist, this is almost inexplicable.

As an alternative explanation, Corbyn makes clear that he believes that the sun (radiance variation, sun-spot activity, and/or solar flares) are the primary cause of climate change; and that ". . . attacks on what the Global Warmers deem as 'solar theory' are the product of disgraceful dishonesty which marks the integrity of the scientific establishment at its lowest level since the Papal Inquisition"; before concluding that integrity ". . . in science, politics and the BBC would be a good idea" (ibid).

Therefore, in addition to disputing that global warming is ongoing, it is very clear that, as an astrophysicist, Corbyn prefers to believe that other objects in our solar system (i.e. the sun and the moon) are the primary cause of any or all climatic variability. Arguably, having taken that decision, he is able to find circumstantial evidence to support that view and, so it seems, equally able to ignore scientific facts that do not.

However, Corbyn has been more forthcoming in the *Comments from Piers* section of the website, which includes links to various articles. For example, in the wake of the Christchurch (New Zealand) earthquake early in 2011, Corbyn stated that:

> [This event followed a world-wide] . . . increase in volcanism and earthquakes in the last year or two and confirms the general statistical fact that [these] tend to occur around solar cycle minima"; and includes a variety of links to supporting data and/or articles; including those linking solar activity with stormy weather (Corbyn 2011a).

However, this does not change the fact that whereas the greenhouse effect is a well-understood mechanism for global warming, there is no obvious causal link between solar activity and volcanism/earthquakes. As such, he appears to overlook the fact that this is therefore equating correlation with causation.

When subsequently interviewed on a radio station in Sydney (NSW), Corbyn made a number of claims including those that (1) it is a scientific fact that CO_2 changes have no climate or weather effect; (2) the world is cooling & heading for mini-ice-age by 2035; and (3) the [ACD] view of reality is as honest as Colonel Gaddafi (Corbyn 2011b). However, even allowing for the probability that he was deliberately being provocative and controversial, it is difficult to understate the scale of the conspiracy that Corbyn is hereby invoking to explain the fact that mainstream scientific opinion and political policy does not give any credence to his views. In fact, it is tempting to compare these with the conspiracy theories circulating in the USA regarding the terrorist attacks on the World Trade Center in New York on 11 September 2001. Including those suggesting the planes were remote controlled and/or that the buildings collapsed as a result of explosive-controlled demolition—in order to provide an excuse for aggressive US foreign policy.

Most recently, in responding to a paper presented on the limited influence that solar activity may have on climate, Corbyn publicly berated the speaker as follows:

> It beggars belief that after you show us these interesting things which make clear how little we know, that you then state the Sun cannot be the driver of Climate Change and instead that it is CO_2! The fact is that there is no evidence in thousands or millions of years of data that CO_2 changes drive any changes in climate and therefore it seems this is more like a religious meeting (Corbyn 2011c).

However, this attempt to equate acceptance of ACD with religious belief is not new. Made recently popular by eminent US physicist, Freeman Dyson (2008), it is intended to ridicule the scientific consensus view in the same way that those that accept the latter ridicule their detractors as "flat-earthers". As did Gordon Brown in advance of the 2009 UNFCCC Meeting in Copenhagen (e.g. as reported in the *Daily Telegraph* newspaper on 4 December 2009, available online at <http://www.telegraph.co.uk/news/politics/6729833/Gordon-Brown-climate-change-sceptics-are-flat-earthers.html> [accessed 07/06/2011].

Such accusations and counter-accusations do not give credence to any point of view nor advance scientific debate. On the contrary, they are more-often associated with those people that, albeit for differing reasons, do not want to debate the facts.

Richard Courtney

In the aftermath of 'Climategate', Meteorologist Richard Courtney submitted written evidence to the Parliamentary Science and Technology Select Committee Inquiry (one of 3 Inquiries undertaken), regarding an email of his (that was amongst those illegally obtained and published on the Internet), which he suggested: ". . . demonstrates that 6 years ago the [CRU] knew the estimates of [mean global temperature—MGT] were worthless and they acted to prevent publication of proof of this" (Courtney 2010). He then went on to argue that attribution studies based on questionable MGT (where cause is assumed and correlation sought) is an argument from ignorance, as follows:

> For example, in the Middle Ages experts said, "We don't know what causes crops to fail: it must be witches: we must eliminate them." Now, experts say, "We don't know what causes global climate change: it must be emissions from human activity: we must

eliminate them." Of course, they phrase it differently saying they can't match historical climate change with known climate mechanisms unless an anthropogenic effect is included. But evidence for this "anthropogenic effect" is no more than the evidence for witches" (ibid).

However, given that there is clear scientific evidence for the warming effect of excess CO_2 in the atmosphere, this is yet another emotive *reductio ad absurdum*[b] argument. Moreover, Courtney does not offer an alternative cause; he seeks only to question the integrity of those with whom he disagrees.

Although it is not the purpose of this present work to adjudicate on who is right or wrong in any respect, it may be pertinent to note that, despite the fact that Courtney's submission was cited as being amongst the majority ". . . from those who stated that the disclosed e-mails confirmed their worries that the climate change orthodoxy has serious flaws and the actions of CRU seriously impugned the integrity of climate change research", the Committee did **not** uphold any such concerns. (See *The disclosure of climate data from the Climatic Research Unit at the University of East Anglia* [Eighth Report of Session 2009-10]). <http://www.publications.parliament.uk/pa/cm200910/cmselect/cmsctech/387/387i.pdf>.

Peter Gill

Peter Gill was a keynote speaker at the *Climate Fools Day*, organised by Piers Corbyn. The advertising for the event indicated that Gill is a "physicist & energy expert" and was to speak about "fictitious 'tipping points' and facts about CO_2" (Weather Action 2010). Earlier in the year, he had come to the attention of the Parliamentary Select Committee investigating the UEA/CRU email scandal because he was the main force behind written evidence submitted thereto by the Institute of Physics (IOP).

Due to the publicity this created, the *Guardian* newspaper journalist David Adam investigated Gill's motives and published his findings on 5 March 2010. David Adam summarised his research into Gill as follows:

> The *Guardian* has established that the [IOP] prepared its evidence, which was highly critical of the CRU scientists, after inviting views from Peter Gill, an IOP official who is head of a company in Surrey called Crestport Services. According to Gill, Crestport offers "consultancy and management support services . . . particularly within the energy and energy intensive industries worldwide", and says that it has worked with "oil and gas production companies including Shell, British Gas, and Petroleum Development Oman". In an article in the newsletter of the IOP south central branch in April 2008, which attempted to downplay the role carbon dioxide plays in global warming, Gill wrote: "If you don't 'believe' in anthropogenic climate change, you risk at best ridicule, but more likely vitriolic comments or even character assassination. Unfortunately, for many people the subject has become a religion, so facts and analysis have become largely irrelevant." In November Gill commented, on the *Times Higher Education* website: "Poor old CRU have been seriously hacked. The emails and other files are all over the internet and include how to hide atmospheric cooling." (Adam 2010).

Based on Adam's research, it would appear that Gill's financial security depends on the continuance of "business as usual" for the fossil fuel exploration and exploitation industry. Furthermore, taking his cue from Freeman Dyson in the USA, Gill equates acceptance of ACD with religious belief; and implies that he is amongst those that believe global warming stopped in 1998.

However, whilst it is common for people on both sides of the ACD "debate" to accuse their opponents of cherry-picking data, the fact remains that sceptics frequently rely upon spatial and temporal variations in weather (see Monbiot 2010b); whilst ignoring that globally observed average temperatures have continued to rise faster than the IPCC predicted; especially in those areas believed to be most sensitive to ACD—namely those at high altitude or latitude (WWF 2008: 3).

Ian Strangeways

Meteorologist, Dr Ian Strangeways (PhD) suspects that systematic measurement error (also known as the "urban heat island" effect) is responsible for indicating (or over-estimating?) that ACD is happening:

> In March 2008, Strangeways told the audience of a Royal Meteorological Society (RMS) meeting that everything in meteorology and climatology comes back to good quality measurements,[c] he pointed out that many meteorological stations are probably not representative of their surrounding areas, and tend disproportionately to be at low-lying, coastal, urban, or airport sites (Strangeways 2008).

Strangeways is the author of several textbooks on meteorology, including *Measuring Global Temperatures: Analysis and Interpretation* in 2009: Within the introductory chapter ("The balance of energy"), the reality of the greenhouse effect is acknowledged, but the burning of fossil fuels is not considered the primary cause:

> In Earth's atmosphere the main greenhouse gases (GHGs) are water vapour (WV), carbon dioxide (CO_2) and methane, with WV being by far the most powerful and prevalent GHG, accounting for about 96% of the total greenhouse effect, CO_2 accounting for 3.6%, and

methane and all the others put together accounting for 1.4% (Strangeways 2009: 8).

Although Strangeways does not explicitly concede that our climate is actually changing, this is implied by the fact that he feels it is necessary to offer an alternative (non-anthropogenic and non-GHG) explanation: "... it appears that variations in the Sun's activity could possibly influence global temperatures . . ."; and even quotes the IPPC as having admitted that "More research to investigate the effects of solar behaviour on climate is needed before the magnitude of solar effects on climate can be stated with certainty" (Strangeways 2009: 17)

(2011) Most recently, Strangeways appears to have re-formatted the same material for presentation in the RMS's Weather journal (Strangeways 2011), which begs the question, what is the RMS position regarding the veracity of ACD? However, from even a brief review of their website, it is clear that they accept that ACD is happening; although it is also clear that they are willing to tolerate dissenting voices.

For example, the talking heads videos all support the consensus view (<http://www.rmets.org/weather/climate/index.php>), whereas alternative views such as those of Strangeways are also simultaneously advertised (<http://www.rmets.org/events/abstract.php?ID=4411>).

Graham Stringer MP

According to the Associate Parliamentary Health Group (APHG), before entering Parliament as a Labour MP in 1997, Graham Stringer had had a career as a Chemist in the plastics industry (APHG).

According to the *Independent* newspaper (31 March 2010), Graham Stringer was the sole member of the Science and Technology Select Committee to distance himself from its decision to clear Professor Phil Jones (CRU) of any scientific malpractice (Connor 2010).

Graham Stringer features regularly on the GWPF website. For example, in an article posted there by Andrew Orlowski in the wake of the 3 inquiries into the UEA/CRU email scandal, Stringer (who made it clear he felt all 3 inquires were either a "white wash" or at very least "inadequate") was quoted as concluding that:

> Vast amounts of money are going to be spent on climate change policy; it's billions and eventually could be trillions. Knowing what is accurate and what is inaccurate is important. I view this as a Parliamentarian for one of the poorest constituencies in the country. Putting up the price of fuel for poor people on such a low level of evidence, hoping it will have the desired effect, is not acceptable. I need to know what's going on (quoted in Orlowski 2010).

From all of this, Stringer's primary motivation appears to be an economic rationalist concern for his constituents. However, his entire thesis is also founded on conspiracy theory; and he clearly does not accept the explanations offered by Professor Phil Jones (CRU) and other climate scientists for those aspects of their behaviour and their written communications that have been widely criticised.

Economists

Roger Bate

In 1994 Roger Bate and Julian Morris (then respectively Director of and Research Fellow within the IEA) set out a critique of the science and economics of climate change and the necessity of policy to deal with it. In many respects, their analysis has been superseded by events (or at least the failure of the UNFCCC process). However, they stated that (1) observed long-term temperature rises have been due to systemic data errors (i.e. the heat island effect); (2) the "enhanced greenhouse effect" (i.e. ACD) was "a highly debatable theory which does not correlate well with empirical data"; and (3) "the effects of increased CO_2 are likely to be beneficial (Bate and Morris 1994: 26-7).

Applying the rules of conventional economics and CBA, they cited the expertise of William Nordhaus in defence of their position that uncertainty over consequences of inaction makes taking action too risky and thus concluded that if ACD is not really happening, "limiting emissions to 1990 levels . . . could reduce global [economic] output by significant amounts" (ibid: 42).

With regard to policy, they favoured research into the feasibility of geoengineering climate stability (i.e. the technological, so-called "end-of-pipe", solution to ACD if it happens) and placed their faith in free markets and price signals as better than models as potential early warning signals of the need for action (ibid: 47).

Sir Ian Byatt

Sir Ian Byatt's contribution is a criticism of the very low discount rate used in the *Stern Review*, because it supposedly results in gross underestimation of the real costs of mitigation of ACD (Byatt 2008). This is a very well-worn argument; one in which many have made personal attacks on Sir Nicholas Stern. However, Stern has explained and justified his position very robustly; pointing out that normal CBA cannot and should not be applied to assessing ACD mitigation costs because scale of the problem is so great; the nature of the threat is non-linear (i.e. positive feedbacks and tipping points); and, therefore, delay could be catastrophic (Stern 2009: 13). William Nordhaus criticised *The Stern Review* on the same grounds. However, as Stern has since pointed out:

> All too many discussions . . . see policy on climate change as a single-investment decision analogous to a new road or a bridge [for which standard] marginal cost-benefit analysis is appropriate . . . For climate change, however, the relevant economics are much more difficult and profound (Stern 2009: 13).

David Henderson

David Henderson's critique of ACD is striking for one main reason, the tendency to preface the word "consensus" with the word "official", the clear implication of which is that this consensus is manufactured by governments for self-serving reasons. However, Henderson cites the cause of the problem as being "the scientific advice provided to them"; that the IPCC is not independent and knows what it is looking for; and/or merely tells governments what they want to hear (Henderson 2008: 72-3). However, with regard to policy, Henderson makes it clear that he favours economy-wide, price-based mechanisms (ibid: 75), which appears to be an admission that ACD is happening.

Lord Lawson

In 2008, Nigel Lawson (former Chancellor of the Exchequer; now Lord Lawson of Blaby) experienced considerable difficulty in finding a publisher for his manuscript for *An Appeal to Reason: A cool look at global warming*. However, it has since proved quite popular and, in 2009, was reprinted in paperback with a new *Afterword* commenting on the response to the book's original publication (which is also discussed below).

However, taking Lawson's work in the order it was published, the first thing to note is the list those who helped to review early drafts of the text: This includes 4 prominent authors associated with the IEA (Samuel Brittan, Ian Byatt, David Henderson, and Julian Morris), Australian geologist Bob Carter (CR), and prominent American sceptic Richard Lindzen (MIT).

In the Introduction to his book, whilst admitting that he is not a scientist, Lawson begins his "cool look at global warming" by equating current concern over ACD with that of the late 1960s and early 1970s regarding fears of "mass global starvation", "running out of natural resources", and of an approaching "disaster of a new ice age" (Lawson 2008: 1). He then makes a very bold but completely unsubstantiated claim that:

> . . . the great majority of those scientists who speak with such certainty and apparent authority about global warming and climate change, are not in fact climate scientists, or indeed earth scientists, of any kind, and thus have no special knowledge to contribute (ibid: 1-2).

Referring to his time "in a not wholly unrelated field" as Energy Secretary in the early 1980s, Lawson states his view that politicians must balance the advice of scientists about "what is happening and why" with an understanding of economics to "tell us what governments should be doing about it". With regard to the latter, he cites the need to consider economic growth forecasting (including energy intensity/demands); cost benefit analysis; global politics; and ethics (ibid: 2).

Chapter 1 is entitled "The Science—and the History", but there is no mention of Svante Arrhenius or Charles Keeling, just another bold statement that "the science of global warming is far from settled" (ibid: 5).[d] There then follows very selective use of global climate data (with no explanation of the complexity of measurements or complicating factors), from which it is clear that he disputes that the climate is still changing (ibid: 7-9).[e]

THE DENIAL OF SCIENCE

Next, Lawson makes clear that he does not deny that carbon dioxide is a GHG but does dispute its importance as such (ibid: 10).[f] Citing the way in which the media tend to report the issue, Lawson then suggests that the IPCC has mutated from "a fact-finding and analytical exercise" into a "politically correct alarmist pressure group" (ibid: 12). Although the "alarmist" label is used frequently throughout the book, this use seems particularly unfair, given the fact that IPCC reports are the product of an extremely robust internal and external review process, which invariably results in very conservative claims being made:

> "The [IPCC] summary describes the existence of global warming as "unequivocal" but leaves out a reference to an accelerated trend in this warming. By excluding statements that provoked disagreement and adhering strictly to data published in peer-reviewed journals, the IPCC has generated a conservative document that may underestimate the changes that will result from a warming world, much as its 2001 report did" (Biello 2007).

The explanation for the inconsistent rise of global average temperatures despite consistent and accelerating anthropogenic GHG emissions given by the IPCC (e.g. the global cooling effect of atmospheric pollution between 1940 and 1975) is dismissed as "pure conjecture" (ibid: 14). Relying heavily upon the analysis of the IEA, Lawson is equally dismissive of the *Stern Review*, (i.e. "essentially a propaganda exercise in support of the UK government's predetermined policy"; and "neither its conclusions nor the arguments on which they are based possess much merit"). As such, Lawson equates the 2006 *Stern Review* with the 2002 "dodgy dossier" on Iraq's Weapons of Mass Destruction, and warns of the danger of "being panicked into what could be disastrously damaging action" (ibid: 21).

Unsurprisingly perhaps, it is clear that Lawson's guiding principle is the last of Henson's propositions (i.e. that we "shouldn't wreck the economy to fix the problem"). However, this book is in fact an attempt to instil doubt in the minds of the reader regarding every facet of research into ACD. As such, it has inadvertently followed Henson's caricature of Contrarianism from start to finish. Furthermore, with regard to discourse analysis, it is the way in which this is done and the language used that is far more significant (e.g. the repeated use of the label "alarmist" or "alarmism" for "proponents of"—or "adherents to"—belief in ACD).[9]

With regard to the *Afterword* added to the 2009 paperback edition of the book, Lawson repeats that he is not competent to pronounce on the validity of the science; and states . . . "I explicitly make it clear that, to be on the safe side, it would be prudent to act as if [the view that ACD is real] were correct . . .". However, in the very next paragraph, he highlights the "three greatest lies" as being (1) that the science is certain and settled; (2) that global warming is actually happening; and (3) that carbon dioxide is a pollutant (Lawson 2009: 107). These are all issues covered in the book but, again, it is the rhetorical language that is particularly telling: Despite his apparent humility over his non-scientific background, he attempts to discredit the science without acknowledging why the majority of scientists take a different view. For example, with regard the latter of these 3 "lies", he fails to note that both the UK and European Environment Agencies treat excess atmospheric carbon dioxide as a pollutant because of its potential to cause acidification of seawater and to disrupt the dynamic equilibrium (between natural carbon sources and sinks); thereby causing ACD (Environment Agency 2011).

Therefore, despite his lack of scientific credentials, Lawson repeats his assertion that global warming "has stopped" (a favourite argument of sceptics). Moreover, he asserts that "true believers" in climate change are the ones "in denial", guilty of "perverse behaviour", and followers of a "new religion" (Lawson 2009: 109). In essence, Lawson has decided what he wants to believe; and is able to find plenty of "evidence" to support

THE DENIAL OF SCIENCE

his pre-determined position; as did the atheist Aldous Huxley (see Huxley, A. (1938), *Ends and Means*. London: Chatto and Windus).

Russell Lewis

Given the title, 'Global Warming: False Alarms' (published on the IEA website in 2007), it is not surprising to find Russell Lewis' critique of the scientific basis for concern regarding ACD, prefaced by a long litany of false alarms that humanity has seen come and go (Lewis 2007: 5-7).[h] As a non-scientist, Lewis' denunciation of science or scientists with whom he does not agree is extraordinary. For example: it is "Government-funded science . . ."; "Dodgy Science . . ." and "Environmental organisations have played their part in corrupting science . . ."; and (ibid: 37, 10, and 35 respectively). Thus, it would appear that Lewis believes governments are motivated to instil fear into their citizens in order to control them (see also Robinson 2008a: 21).

Lewis begins his 'Global Alarmism' contribution to Robinson's 2008 volume, by linking alarmism with a desire to be "cool", citing such varied dignitaries as Tony Blair, Sir David King, Archbishop of Canterbury and James Lovelock as unwitting victims (Lewis 2008: 26). He goes on to suggest that Rachel Carson was an alarmist because DDT is not dangerous (ibid: 33-5); and that acid rain does not damage trees (ibid: 35-6). Having re-stated the now familiar litany of supposed false alarms, Lewis cites Michael Crichton's belief that environmentalism "has become a kind of fundamentalist religion . . . which cannot be moved by argument or factual evidence"; and concludes that, if so, global environmental scares will recede only when environmental bigotry yields to honest scientific inquiry" (Lewis 2008: 40). As such, environmentalists are variously presented as being "cool", credulous, superstitious, bigoted, and intellectually dishonest, which is a curious mix to say the least.

Alister McFarquhar

According to a very well-referenced article on the De-Smog Blog disinformation database, created by James Hoggan (author of *Climate Cover Up*), Alister McFarquhar is an economist with links to the ASI; is a signatory to the *Manhattan Declaration on Climate Change*; and:

- has not published any research articles in peer-reviewed journals (according to a search of 22,000 academic journals); although a Google search yielded an apparently co-authored paper, entitled 'Agriculture and the State: British Policy in a World Context', published in the US Foreign Affairs Journal in 1977;
- is listed as a signatory to a 2007 open letter to United Nations Secretary General Ban Ki-Moon (that describes global warming as "a natural phenomenon that has affected humanity through the ages," and describes CO_2 as a "non-polluting gas that is essential to plant photosynthesis");
- signed a 2006 Open Letter to [then Canadian] Prime Minister Stephen Harper recommending that the government stall any action on climate policy because the "climate changes all the time due to natural causes"; and
- appears as one of 20 economists on a list of over 400 "prominent climate scientists" that deny global warming published by Senator James Inhofe (De-Smog Blog—*Alister McFarquhar*).

Based on the above evidence, McFarquhar does not mind being wrongly identified as a climate scientist and, as such, has no qualms about promoting sceptical views to prominent politicians, and perpetuating confusion over natural climate variability and ACD.

Julian Morris

As do many other authors associated with the IEA, Julian Morris disputes the fact that the "science is settled", which he calls a "falsehood" (Morris 2008: 132). Indeed, taken together with the assertion that environmentalists are treating sceptics as heretics, there is almost an air of moral superiority in evidence (in as much as heretics such as Galileo were eventually exonerated). If not, at very least, this is an attempt to question the nature of truth itself. It is also interesting to note that Morris and the IPN were identified in the Houses of Parliament (on 8 February 2005) by Norman Baker MP (then Liberal Democrat Shadow Secretary of State for the Environment, Environment, Food & Rural Affairs) as having links to ExxonMobil and, of Morris, he said "there is an ulterior motive behind his denial of climate change" (Hansard 2005: c.1355).

Alan Peacock

Alan Peacock suggests that "the raising of barriers . . . to entry into critical discussion of the science of climate change" is equivalent to the way in which "established religions view heresy"; and is very critical of "an uncritical acceptance of this new conventional wisdom" (Peacock 2008: 114). Peacock then draws analogies between religious concepts (such as sin and salvation; prophecy and punishment) and aspects of the environmentalist message that climate change is real, we are to blame, and failure to change our ways will result in annihilation (ibid 115-21). Citing the striking claim that "environmentalism is replacing Marxism as the ideological opponent of liberalism" (attributed to Vaclav Klaus), Peacock says that international attempts to co-ordinate legislative action to mitigate ACD are indeed ideologically-driven; and that we should therefore "be wary of the dangers to individual freedom inherent in the present consensus . . ." (ibid: 130).

Colin Robinson

In his introduction to the collection of essays by fellow economists that he compiled and edited, Colin Robinson uses J.K. Galbraith's term "conventional wisdom" as a label for "the prevailing view that damaging climate change is in progress and will become worse in the future" and, in the process, equates Galbraith's concept of conventional wisdom with "ideas notable *not* for their intellectual content but *because* they have become acceptable and are what people want to hear" [emphasis added] (Robinson 2008a: 19). He therefore suggests that the leaders of this "movement" suppress dissenting views because "the only debate they want is about the choice among the different forms of centralised action they believe is required to deal with the problems they foresee"; and repeatedly refers to this view as "the damaging climate change hypothesis" (ibid: 20-1).

Robinson also highlights a common thread amongst all the contributions to his book, which is that "the climate change movement has religious overtones which lead to intolerance and could, through inducing drastic centralised action, bring about restrictions on freedom" (ibid:21).

Although there is no doubt about the nature of Robinson's fears regarding this "conventional wisdom", he does not offer any explanation as to why such an unpalatable message would be one that "people want to hear". However, be that as it may, the message Robinson clearly wishes to convey is that we probably do not have a problem but, if we do, we should not wreck the economy to fix it. Although Robinson would clearly dispute it (ibid: 25), this appears to be Contrarianism cunningly disguised as Economic Rationalism.

Robinson's second contribution to his IEA publication discusses "the problems inherent in apocalyptic forecasting and [the centralised] planning that normally accompanies it"; "the weaknesses of climate change modelling"; "the property rights question that underlies the climate change problem"; and "appropriate policy responses to present-day fears of [ACD] and its consequences" (Robinson 2008b: 42). As such, this contribution appears to concede that ACD is happening but not that any action is required: "Once the apocalyptic forecast is seen in context [of previous false alarms] and the likely failures of government action are recognised, the case for urgent, centralised action . . . seems much less convincing . . . (ibid: 66).

In other words, "leave it to the market" as John Dryzek put it (2005: 121)—Economic Rationalism.

Journalists

Christopher Booker

What Booker actually said was this:

> Next Friday is the first anniversary of the leaking of the "Climategate" emails—the correspondence of a small group of scientists at the heart of the UN's Intergovernmental Panel on Climate Change (IPPC). By exposing their manipulation of data and suppression of dissent, these called their reputation as disinterested scientists seriously into question . . . Next month sees the anniversary of the Copenhagen conference—the largest ever held, with upwards of 100,000 people present—which collapsed in an acrimonious shambles, without the treaty that would have landed the world with the biggest bill in history. This was followed by all those scandals surrounding the IPCC itself, hitherto regarded as the supreme authority on global warming. It emerged that the most recent IPCC report was riddled with errors, and that many of its more alarming predictions were based,

not on proper science, but on claims dreamed up by environmental activists (Booker 2010a).

N.B. He also exaggerates the significance of errors in IPCC reports and accuses them of being unscientific and alarmist, when the truth of the matter (Biello 2007) is the exact opposite.

In December 2010, with the UK in the grip of some of the coldest weather on record, Booker suggested that between "their tequilas and lavish meals paid for by the world's taxpayers", delegates at the UNFCCC meeting in (the "sun-drenched Mexican holiday resort of") Cancun were being told that everyone should be issued with a "carbon ration card [. . . that will . . .] halt all Western economic growth for 20 years" (Booker 2010b).

On the subject of possible geoengineering solutions, such as putting giant mirrors in space, seeding the oceans with iron filings (to promote algal growth), and carbon capture and storage, he describes these as either "ritualised scaremongering", or (quite possibly correctly) as "make-believe" and "fanciful"; and concluded by saying that all of this is therefore ". . . one of the greatest collective flights from reality in the history of the human race" (ibid).

Although content to claim extreme cold weather as evidence that ACD is not happening, Booker is nonetheless dismissive of studies indicating that it may be making extreme weather events (such as flooding) more likely:

> As the great global warming scare continues to crumble, attention focuses on all those groups that have a huge interest in keeping it alive. Governments look on it as an excuse to raise billions of pounds in taxes. Wind farm developers make fortunes from the hidden subsidies we pay through our electricity bills. A vast academic industry receives more billions for concocting the bogus science that underpins the

scare. Carbon traders hope to make billions from corrupt schemes based on buying and selling the right to emit CO_2. But no financial interest stands to make more from exaggerating the risks of climate change than the re-insurance industry, which charges retail insurers for "catastrophe cover", paid for by all of us through our premiums (Booker 2011).

In 'A personal note from the author' at the back of his 2009 book, *The Real Global Warming Disaster,* Booker explains how he became interested in what he sees as the excesses of environmental alarmism, as a result of reading an article in 2003 about Danish wind farms (where night-time electricity was exported to Norway; from where it had to be imported when there was no wind). This led him to become chairman of a local action group protesting against plans for local wind turbines; and to wonder about the motivation of those in favour of such schemes (due to what Booker perceives to be unfounded fears of an approaching ACD catastrophe). As a result, one of the first books he read was *Unstoppable Global Warming* (2006) by the ubiquitous Cold War physicist, Dr Fred Singer, followed by books by Richard Lindzen and Patrick Michaels (2009: 353-5).

Given the primary influence of Singer (2006), Booker's starting point appears to be that climate change is a natural occurrence so we should get used to it. However, as is clear from the subtitle of his own book (*Is the Obsession with 'Climate Change' Turning Out to be the Most Costly Scientific Blunder in History*) his greatest concern is an economic one (i.e. that the problem is not sufficiently great to warrant drastic action and excessive cost as currently proposed).

This is therefore more Cornucopianism than anything else.

James Delingpole

Increasingly sceptical over time, on the publication of the Russell Report, he blogged:

> So the Sir Muir Russell inquiry into Climategate was, pretty much, a whitewash. But then we'd already guessed that. The danger with all these official cover-ups . . . is that they distract from the main point [which is that] under the terms of the 2008 Climate Change Act we are the only country in the world legally committed to making swinging reductions in CO2, the harmless trace gas which helps plants grow and which we really need more of not less in order to soften the blow of the imminent global cooling. How much is this lunacy going to cost us? The figure which used to be quoted was £18 billion per annum. Apparently this has now more than doubled. The new figure our glorious Coalition intends to squander—every single year for the next 40 years—is £50 billion, all in order to deal with a problem that doesn't actually exist (Delingpole 2010).

However, there is strong evidence to suggest that Delingpole's scepticism, which existed before Climategate, is not based on economic or scientific criticism, it is ideological: In a remarkably frank interview with Sir Paul Nurse, as broadcast on a BBC *Horizon* programme entitled 'Meet the Climate Sceptics' on 24 January 2011, Delingpole admits that:

- he believes concern about climate change is being driven by a "political agenda" seeking "control" over people;
- "the peer review process has been perhaps irretrievably corrupted" [i.e. (presumably) 'discredited'?] by Climategate;
- Science should now be assessed by "peer-to-peer review" over the Internet by thousands and thousands

of people including "people like me that haven't got a scientific background" (Delingpole 2011).

However, when Nurse queried the legitimacy of this [non-peer review] process, by asking if he would or could read peer-reviewed scientific literature, Delingpole's response was remarkable: "It is not my job to sit down and read peer-reviewed science papers because . . . I haven't got the scientific expertise . . . I am an interpreter of interpretations . . ." (ibid).

Thus it would seem that, to Delingpole, ACD is a left-wing global conspiracy conducted by environmentalist "watermelons" (i.e. green on the outside but red on the inside),[i] which can only be prevented if free-thinking individuals resist being duped by the consensus into giving up their liberty.

If this fits anywhere within the typology proposed then it must be considered as 100% ideologically-driven Contrarianism.

Martin Durkin

Martin Durkin was the director of Channel 4's *The Great Global Warming Swindle* documentary first broadcast in 2007 and, before that, *Against Nature* in 1997, which characterised environmentalist ideology as "unscientific, irrational and anti-humanist" (i.e. presumably ecocentric or misanthropic); and was the subject of numerous complaints (Ofcom 1998). However, immediately after being broadcast in 1997, Monbiot highlighted the links between Durkin, the Living Marxism magazine, and the Revolutionary Communist Party (RCP), which was then a spin-off from the British Communist Party). Monbiot demonstrated how the programme was, in effect, a presentation of RCP's political agenda:

> Greens, both the series and Living Marxism maintain, present themselves as radicals, but are really doom-mongering imperialists, engaged in

the deification of Nature and the rejection of human progress. Global warming is nothing to worry about, while sustainable development is a conspiracy against people. Greens have plotted with the film industry to make science terrifying. Genetic engineering and human cloning are not to be feared but cherished, as they will liberate humanity from nature (Monbiot 1997).

Despite this, Durkin does not seem to have accepted (or learnt from) the criticism because the broadcast of his 2007 documentary prompted even more complaints and was heavily criticised for many things including (again) his misleading contributors as to the nature of the programme being made and misrepresenting their known views (Ofcom 2007). As an example of Durkin's views, his voice-over (narration) for the programme began with the following:

> Everywhere you are told that man-made climate change is proved beyond doubt. But you are being told lies . . . This is a story of how a theory about climate turned into a political ideology . . . it is the story of the distortion of a whole area of science . . . it is the story of how a political campaign turned into a bureaucratic bandwagon . . . (ibid).

Andrew Montford

Despite the title and focus of the book on the MBH98 graph, Montford's conspiracy theory is actually rooted in the foundation of the World Meteorological Organisation (WMO) in 1977 and the first World Climate Conference in Geneva in 1979. Montford chooses to see something sinister in the fact that, having been instructed to review the state of knowledge and tell governments what the implications are for humanity, the Conference issued a '*Call to Nations*' (for full advantage to be taken of man's knowledge of climate . . . and for potential manmade changes to climate to be foreseen and prevented). Here, according to Montford, the scientists supposedly saw ". . . a source of funding and influence without end" (Montford 2010a: 21-2). With regard to the MBH98 graph itself, Montford also makes it clear at the outset that this was the inevitable product of a much earlier decision that the Medieval Warm Period (MWP) needed to "disappear":

> Climate science wanted big funding and big political action and that was going to require definitive evidence. In order to strengthen the arguments for the current warming being unprecedented, there was going to have to be a major study, presenting unimpeachable evidence that the [MWP] was a chimera (ibid 2010a: 30). [j]

Thus, an accountant set out to summarise attempts by a mining consultant and an economist to discredit the work of a team of multi-disciplinary scientists. As such, it does not seem unreasonable to question the motives of the non-scientists involved. Why do they find it necessary to question the integrity of the scientists? Once again, the answer (a denial of responsibility for ACD) accords with Aaronovitch's explanation for conspiracy theories.

In the topsy-turvy sceptical world that people like Delingpole and Montford inhabit, it might not be that surprising that the GWPF would ask Montford to write a report into what they feel were 3 totally inadequate inquiries into the scientific research being undertaken by the UEA/CRU. Unsurprisingly, therefore, Montford finds evidence of a state-sponsored conspiracy to provide an excuse to tax people more heavily:

> With the government embarking upon a radical decarbonisation programme, global warming is one of the most important questions facing the people of the UK today . . . While attempts to hide the truth from the

public might have worked in the past, they simply wilt under this kind of scrutiny (Montford 2010b: 6).

Given the underwhelming response to this report, it would seem that, in reality, few people believed him: Montford's GWPF report was considered in a further review of the matter by the House of Commons Science and Technology Committee (The Reviews into the University of East Anglia's Climatic Research Unit's E-mails: First Report of Session 2010-11), which concluded (25 January 2011) that:

> The disclosure of data from CRU has been traumatic and challenging for all involved. While we have some reservations about the reviews which UEA commissioned, the key point is that they have made a number of constructive recommendations. In our view it is time to make the changes and improvements recommended and with greater openness and transparency move on (p.4).

<http://www.publications.parliament.uk/pa/cm201011/cmselect/cmsctech/444/444.pdf> [accessed 10/06/2011].

Brendan O'Neill

Brendan O'Neill is the editor of the multi-faceted, online magazine website *Spiked*, which describes itself as:

> ... an independent online phenomenon dedicated to raising the horizons of humanity by waging a culture war of words against misanthropy, priggishness, prejudice, luddism, illiberalism and irrationalism in all their ancient and modern forms. Spiked is endorsed by free-thinkers such as John Stuart Mill and Karl Marx, and hated by the narrow-minded such as Torquemada and Stalin. Or it would be, if they were lucky enough to be around to read it (Spiked 2011).

In his discussion of left-wing scepticism, Hamilton (2010a: 113-5) highlights the links between the Revolutionary Communist Party (RCP), *Living Marxism* magazine, and the *Spiked* website, which clearly does not deny its Marxist roots; but does try to broaden its appeal through the use of humour. Therefore, irrespective of the extent to which O'Neill is still a Marxist, it is nevertheless surprising that he is given a platform on the websites of *The Telegraph* and the GWPF and many others.[k] Given these links, it is perhaps not surprising that O'Neill should have defended Durkin's 2007 documentary on the *Spiked* website,[l] which Hamilton characterises as ". . . an endorsement of the film's anti-environmental claims veiled by appeals to the [human] right to dissent" (ibid: 115).

Indeed, this would appear to have been O'Neill's intent because, a few months earlier he had said, "Whatever the truth about our warming planet, it is clear there is a tidal wave of intolerance in the debate about climate change which is eroding free speech and melting rational debate." (O'Neill 2006). As such, in this article (subtitled 'The demonisation of "climate change denial" is an affront to open and rational debate'), O'Neill was objecting to the term "denial" because of its associations with "holocaust denial" and with people who believe that the Earth is flat, *etc*.

In the wake of extremely cold weather in the UK winter of 2010/11, O'Neill referred to previous warnings that ACD would bring an end to snowy winters in the UK as "unadulterated nonsense", but conceded that:

> If it is mad to cite every change in the weather as proof that Earth is doomed, then it's probably also unwise to dance around in the slushy white stuff in the belief that it proves that all environmental scientists are demented liars (O'Neill 2011a).

Unfortunately, he then added:

> But the world of difference between expert predictions (hot hell) and our real experiences (freezing nightmare) is a powerful symbol of the distance that now exists between the apocalypse-fantasising elites and the public. What it really shows is the extent to which the politics of global warming is driven by an already existing culture of fear. It doesn't matter what The Science (as greens always refer to it) does or doesn't reveal: campaigners will still let their imaginations run riot, biblically fantasising about droughts and plagues, because theirs is a fundamentally moralistic outlook rather than a scientific one. It is their disdain for mankind's planet-altering arrogance that fuels their global-warming fantasies . . . [which] are better understood as elite moral porn rather than sedate risk analysis (ibid).

However, five years on from 2006, O'Neill was also still peddling the anti-censorship message; albeit possibly a little more explicit about his own point of view:

> Who would seriously quibble with [Johnny Ball's] critique of the idea that in 39 or 40 years' time earth will no longer be able to sustain human life, and his concern that teaching such guff in schools is "frightening schoolchildren to an alarming degree"? . . . But then, when it comes to climate change orthodoxy—the planet's getting hotter, it's mankind's fault, only eco-austerity will save us—it doesn't matter if your challenge is wacky or well-informed. It will still be treated as suspect, as the ravings of a crazed mind or part of an oil-funded dastardly plot. No dissent can be tolerated . . . It's like an Inquisition in reverse. Where the first inquisitors sometimes punished those who promoted rationalism, today's "eco-inquisitors" attack those who question their narrow view of what's rational. Indeed, chief scientist John Beddington this month called on the scientific community to be

"grossly intolerant" of anyone who promotes what he decrees to be "bad science" (O'Neill 2011b).

Melanie Philips

Melanie Phillips is a British journalist and author who has spent most of her working life (1977-2001) working for the left-of-centre *Guardian* newspaper. In 2003, Andy Beckett wrote an article therein charting Philips' life-long drift (as he at least sees it) from liberalism to conservatism, in which he described Phillips as ". . . a dynamic young reporter [in 1977] who championed the poor and shared the values of the liberal left. But today, Melanie Phillips is a Daily Mail columnist who despairs at the moral decay of British society and espouses traditional values" (Beckett 2003).

Furthermore, although it is unlikely he was seeking to be complimentary, Beckett also wrote that: "Phillips' trademarks of social concern, pessimism about modern Britain and seemingly absolute certainty have made her—against stiff competition—arguably the most high-profile and prolific British pundit on moral and political matters" (ibid).

According to her own website, Phillips "read English at St Anne's College, Oxford before training as a journalist . . . she started writing her [*Guardian*] column in 1987, taking it to the *Observer* and then the *Sunday Times* before starting to write for the *Daily Mail* in December 2001" (Phillips 2010).

Acknowledging the criticism of others, her biography notes that although described as "a conservative by her opponents, she prefers to think of herself as defending authentic liberal values against the attempt to destroy western culture from within" (ibid).

It would appear that ever since moving to the *Daily Mail*, Phillips has taken to repeatedly attacking climate science and ACD as a politically motivated scam:

> But there is simply no scientific evidence to support this theory. Indeed, many of the scientific claims made by the global warming industry are demonstrably wrong . . . Global warming is a scam . . . Computer modelling is in general a dubious scientific tool. When it comes to climate change, it uses partial data to transform flawed hypotheses into prophecy. It is of little more use than a [sic] ouija board (Phillips 2002a).

The use of pseudo-religious rhetoric is undoubtedly deliberate mockery. However, the both the conspiracy theory and the ideological reasoning that makes her position necessary are both very clearly stated:

> The brutal explanation is that [scientists] don't get grant money or the approval needed for promotion unless their work supports the politically motivated theory of the times . . . But why is global warming so popular politically? The short answer is that [it is] a doctrine which declares that industrialisation and globalisation are enemies of humanity . . . The longer answer is that the roots of the environmental movement go back to Thomas Malthus . . . After the Nazis took this theory to its grotesque conclusion, eugenics went deep underground and re-emerged under the cover of the world-wide birth control and environmental movements . . . (ibid)

Writing in the wake of the 2002 UN Conference on Sustainable Development in Johannesburg, Phillips said:

> There is no doubt that we need to clean the environment, and to do this we need to prevent pollution. But the fact remains that there is simply

> no credible evidence that global warming is happening, or if it is that man-made carbon dioxide is the culprit . . . Global warming is no more than an ideological scam being used to attack the west from within. The Green movement is deeply reactionary and anti-human . . . In the 16th century, the extreme hardships and destruction caused by global cooling prompted widespread pogroms against witches . . . Five centuries on, a similar witch-hunt is on over climate change. This time, the targets are capitalism, western values and America; but the principal victims are the world's poor—and truth itself. (Phillips 2002b).

In the same article she also managed to blame "Greens" for our inability to decouple environmental degradation from economic development, as follows:

> For this summit is exposing the contradictions at the heart of 'sustainable development' in an argument which the Greens are losing. The poor peoples of the third world are saying that only development will rescue them from poverty, malnutrition and disease. This is, of course, an anathema to the Greens, whose 'sustainability' analysis rests on the premise that western development is killing the planet. Having been forced onto the moral back foot, the Greens are even more desperate to prove that global warming and climate catastrophe are the fault of western man (ibid).

In 2004, criticising the then government's Chief Scientific Adviser, Sir David King, for an article published in *Science*, (warning us that the ten hottest years on record started in 1991, that global warming is causing the ice caps to melt and the seas to rise, and that mankind's activities in producing carbon dioxide have been proved to be the cause) she said:

> With all due respect to Sir David's eminence, every one of these claims is utter garbage. What science actually tells us is that we just don't know whether global warming is happening and, if it is, why. Much of the research behind this theory is specious, anti-historical and scientifically illiterate . . . Far from being proved, the claim of man-made global warming is a global fraud . . . Indeed, global warming has little to do with science and everything to do with politics . . . Since the global warming prediction emerged in the late 1980s, climate science funding has gone through the roof . . . So global warming has become big business. This is ironic. For it is yet another variation of left-wing, anti-American, anti-west ideology which goes hand in hand with anti-globalisation and the belief that everything done by the industrialised world is wicked . . . (Phillips 2004).

In the run-up to the US Presidential Election campaign of 2008, she criticised Republican candidate John McCain for his environmental policies: "Anyone who endorses, as he does, the man-made global warming scam displays an alarming absence of judgment and common sense" (Phillips 2008).

Attacking Jonathon Porritt for suggesting that unrestrained population growth and use of the Earth's environmental resources could be problematic, she described him as "not so much a friend of the earth as an enemy of the human race" (Phillips 2009).

Furthermore, she insisted that to seek to curb our natural instinct to reproduce on the basis of his supposed superior insight into the needs of our world, ". . . is not just monumental arrogance—it is also the delusion of totalitarian tyrants from Stalin to Hitler to Mao" (ibid).

Tim Worstall

Tim Worstall describes himself as an "Englishman who has failed at many things . . ." who has turned to writing as ". . . the last refuge of many who could make a living no other way"; whose work has ". . . been known to turn up in *The Times*, the book pages of the *Daily Telegraph* and the *Philadelphia Inquirer* . . .", and who has ". . . been a long term contributor to [the online magazine] *TCS Daily* and also blogs for *The Business* and the *Adam Smith Institute*" (Worstall 2007).

In 2010, Worstall wrote *Chasing Rainbows: Economic Myths, Environmental Facts*, which examines what we should be doing "to avoid, curtail or adapt to global warming" (ibid), which:

> . . . looks at the commonly held beliefs about what we should do to avoid, curtail or adapt to global warming and compares them to what we should actually be doing. This is not an argument about the science: Worstall leaves that entirely to others to debate. Rather, he asks what guides and indications we can draw from the economics already embedded in such pronouncements as the IPCC reports and the Stern Review. The answers will shock some: globalisation is part of the cure for climate change. Recycling of some things certainly saves resources but of domestic waste actually squanders them. Creating 'green jobs' is not a benefit but a cost of our actions. We don't need to limit economic growth, quite the opposite, it's part of the solution, and the finite nature of the physical world is not a binding limit upon such growth. (Independent Minds 2010).

According to the ASI, the book . . . "takes on the global warming alarmists on their own terms, accepting the IPPC's science, and uses the logic of economics to argue that the ends that environmentalists want is best achieved through more globalisation and freer markets, not government interventions like cap-and-trade" (ASI 2010).

Politicians

Graham Brady

In an article in the *Independent* newspaper, entitled 'Cameron hit by Tory backlash on environment', Andrew Grice quotes a variety of Conservative MPs expressing concern over policy to mitigate ACD, including Graham Brady:

> "There is some room for debate about why the climate is changing and the best ways of tackling it. It is a good idea to reduce carbon emissions, but I would not want to see the whole economy destroyed in the process. There is a balance to be struck" (as quoted in Grice 2009).

Douglas Carswell

Douglas Carswell is an outspoken backbench MP who was clearly so impressed by reading Ian Plimer's book that he decided to blog about it (criticising Prof John Schellnhuber of the Potsdam Institute for labelling Americans as being 'ignorant about climate change'), as follows:

> Perhaps we should send the Americans copies of Prof Ian Plimer's book on the subject . . . to enlighten them? . . . If we did, those 'climate illiterate' Americans would learn how some scientists are of the view that: FACT 1: Global temperatures are not determined by the amount of CO_2 in the atmosphere. FACT 2: The amount of CO_2 in the atmosphere is largely determined by geology—and human activity has only

a very marginal effect . . . But surely, good science is not about the weight of opinion, but about the weight of fact and evidence? . . . In the free market of ideas, expect a correction soon (Douglas Carswell's Blog 29/09/2009).

A few days later, he began another post on his blog by saying, "The lunatic 'consensus' on man-made climate change is starting to break down" (ibid—12/10/2009).

However, as a result of this latter comment, Carswell was criticised by many and got himself into his local newspaper, the *Clacton Gazette*, which quoted him as having said:

"I have thought long and hard about it and in my view the climate is not changing because of human activity . . . We know that it was a lot warmer in the middle ages. In Essex, we know a variety of grapes were grown, it was that much warmer . . . I read a book this summer which details less than half of one percent of all CO2 in the atmosphere and surface of the earth is caused by man" (as quoted in *Clacton Gazette* of 23/10/2009).

Christopher Chope

In the final debate on the Climate Change Bill (28 October 2008) in the House of Commons, one of the three rebels, Christopher Chope said:

The issue that we are discussing needs to be put into context. A paper that PricewaterhouseCoopers produced, entitled "The world in 2050", projects that the United Kingdom will produce only 1.2% of global emissions in 2050—without the increased targets in the Bill and without including emissions from shipping and aviation. We must take that into consideration.

> Even if we eliminated that 1.2%, would it make any difference to the world? I do not think that it would—indeed, the burdens on our economy would be even more enormous than they are already likely to be, as my right hon. Friend the Member for Hitchin and Harpenden (Mr. Lilley) explained so well (Hansard 2008b: c.769).

Philip Davies

Philip Davies is one of a number of Conservative MPs who has made sceptical contributions to parliamentary debates, for example:

> We appear to have gone down a road whereby people's ability to exercise free speech on certain subjects is being undermined, and there is no greater example of that at the moment than climate change. People have jumped on to that particular bandwagon with religious zeal, rather than looking at the issue from a purely objective perspective. Of course we all care about the future of our planet and the legacy that we leave our children and grandchildren-nobody doubts the importance of that—but the question is how effective the measures taken are in tackling any problem that there may be. It is no good our trying to do something completely disproportionate that disproportionately affects our economy and the quality of life of the people of this country, with no overall benefit to the world as a whole, anyway (Hansard 2007: c.1020).

More recently, in an article in the *Independent* newspaper, entitled 'Cameron hit by Tory backlash on environment', Andrew Grice cited a variety of Conservative MPs as expressing concern over policy to mitigate ACD, including Davies:

> I would like to see some proper cost-benefit analysis [at Copenhagen] on the impact on the economy, rather than this charge towards trying to be trendy and to please the environmental lobby. Everyone has gone completely mad on this. It has taken on the hallmarks of a religion rather than a policy issue. Anyone who says 'hang on a minute' is completely decried and treated like a Holocaust denier (as quoted in Grice 2009).

David Davis

On the eve of the UNFCCC Meeting in Copenhagen in 2009, former Shadow Home Secretary and candidate for Conservative Party leader, David Davis MP wrote an article for the *Independent* newspaper (published the same day as that by Grice), in which he said:

> The row about whether global warming exists gets even more virulent. The case is not helped by the fact that the planet appears to have been cooling, not warming, in the last decade . . . Today, the economic climate makes people question whether we can afford the expense of these policies. The UK's environmental policy has a long-term price tag of about £55bn, before taking into account the impact on economic growth . . . The ferocious determination to impose hair-shirt policies on the public—taxes on holiday flights, or covering our beautiful countryside with wind turbines that look like props from War of the Worlds—would cause a reaction in any democratic country (Davis 2009).

Daniel Hannan

Daniel Hannan MEP is often cited as a sceptic but it would probably be more accurate to describe him as an agnostic. In a wide-ranging post (dated 2 December 2009) on his own blog, hosted by the *Telegraph* newspaper's website, he makes his position quite clear:

> We all tend, unconsciously, to press new data into our existing *Weltanschauung* . . . Reading the leaked [UEA/CRU] emails, it seems pretty clear that their authors genuinely believe that the world is getting hotter as a result of human activity. Having formed this view, they instinctively dismiss evidence that doesn't fit it . . . The case for anthropogenic global warming was, as far as I can understand, slightly more convincing a decade ago than it is today, with global temperatures having recently dropped. Having reached sincere and considered opinions in the 1990s, and having built careers on that basis, some of the Rio-Kyoto-Copenhagen crowd understandably find it awkward to re-examine their assumptions (Hannan 2009).

Hannan therefore acknowledges the possibility that both ACD "believers" and "deniers" may be afflicted by cognitive dissonance, he gives equal weight to the arguments of both and ignores the fact that the vast majority of (not just "some") climate scientists are convinced (by mounting evidence) that ACD is a reality. However, he continues:

> Does this happen among on the other side, too? Yes, undoubtedly. Just as those who already believed in more regulation, more government, supra-nationalism and higher taxes honestly think that carbon emissions are overheating the planet, so libertarians and small government types honestly think that the whole thing is [rubbish]. Each faction, convinced of its own

sincerity, distrusts the motives of the other . . . All of which makes it almost impossible for the layman to reach a confident view. It's not just the interpretation of the facts that is disputed, but the facts themselves. Leave aside the argument over CO_2: there isn't even any agreement over how much the world is heating. So where do I stand? With Peter Lilley, I suppose. I think the world is warming (I especially dislike the phase "climate change denial": no one, as far as I'm aware, is positing climate stasis). And it may well be that human activity is playing some part in the process, although probably not to the degree claimed by some climate change professionals . . . If this makes me a "sceptic", in the literal sense of wanting to question things, fine. But I resent the notion that it somehow makes me anti-environment (Hannan 2009).

Roger Helmer

In a speech to the European Parliament on 4 February 2009, Roger Helmer MEP claimed, in characteristically robust terms, that the EU was:

> . . . planning to spend unimaginable sums of money on mitigation measures which will simply not work, and by damaging our economies will deny us the funds we need to address real environmental problems. As a British journalist, Christopher Booker, has remarked, global warming alarmism is the greatest collective flight from reality in human history (Helmer 2009).

According to Andrew Grice in the *Independent*, Helmer has even accused the Church of England of having "abandoned religious faith entirely and taken up the new religion of climate change alarmism instead" (quoted in Grice 2009).

Martin Lack

Peter Lilley

On 5 November 2009 (just prior to the UNFCCC Meeting in Copenhagen), Lilley said:

> The science is not a fairy tale. The basic science is that if the amount of CO_2 in the atmosphere is doubled . . . that will increase the surface temperature of the atmosphere by 1°C . . . If that higher temperature were to result in more water vapour in the atmosphere, which it does not seem to have done, that would raise the temperature by another 2°C . . . The Government and the alarmists have to concoct a lot of feedbacks that so far have not manifested themselves to predict that in future we will see far higher rises in temperature from a given increase in CO_2 than we have in the past. I am neither a denier of the science nor an alarmist (Lilley 2009b).

However, in the same debate, Lilley went on to refer (at considerable length) to a dispute within the American Physical Society (APS), 160 members of which had issued an open letter rebuking their leaders for issuing a statement describing evidence for ACD as "incontrovertible". Lilley quoted from their letter as follows:

> . . . while substantial concern has been expressed that emissions may cause significant climate change, measured or reconstructed temperature records indicate that 20th-21st century changes are neither exceptional nor persistent, and the historical and geological records show many periods warmer than today . . . Current climate models appear insufficiently reliable to properly account for natural and anthropogenic contributions to past climate change, much less project climate change (cited in Lilley 2009b).

John Maples

John Maples is another Conservative backbencher willing to be publicly sceptical. In an early debate on the Climate Change Bill (9 June 2008) he said:

> Until a couple of months ago, I was happily riding this consensus and basically accepted the received wisdom. I thought that it was probably being exaggerated a bit, but then people usually do that in making a case. However, I then made the mistake of reading a few books and quite a lot of analysis, particularly of [the Stern Review]. I do not believe that the science is anything like as settled as the proponents of the Bill are making out. In fact, the scientists hedge their predictions with an awful lot of qualifications and maybes that those who invoke them often omit. The science is a bit like medicine in the 1850s. The scientists are scratching the surface of something that they do not really understand, but no doubt will. They are probably on to something, but nothing like the whole story. What they say does not justify any of the apocalyptic visions that we have heard set out (Hansard 2008a: c.103).

John Redwood

According to his own website, the Rt Hon John Redwood MP (i.e. also a former Cabinet Minister in the Thatcher government) has a business background and, "has been a director of NM Rothschild merchant bank and chairman of a quoted industrial PLC" (Redwood 2006).

In response to the first broadcast of the Channel 4 documentary, *The Great Global Warming Swindle*, in March 2007, Redwood blogged:

> Things are not entirely as the "consensus" supposes. A recent news item has told us visits to Mars by space probes detect "global" warming there . . . leading people to ask if the sun is currently hotting up affecting all of the solar system. We do need to know more about cloud formation, water vapour, sun flares and spots and volcanic activity to be sure what is causing the phase of warming that started in 1975 after 35 years of cooling. I have always thought we should remain sceptical about all scientific theories, for that is the way that science advances by constantly submitting theories to test. Meanwhile we are living in a period when things are warming up, so we should manage any unhelpful consequences of that and welcome the good effects it will have (Redwood 2007).

More recently, in a blog post entitled 'Those climate projections in full', Redwood lists a number of assertions made my climate scientists, but chooses to focus on the debate about what causes extreme weather events; and mockingly concludes that, "when the weather goes in the wrong direction, it is just weather and not climate" (Redwood 2010).

Andrew Tyrie

Andrew Tyrie, the third of the 3 rebel Conservatives, made his opposition to the Climate Change Bill very clear on 9 June 2008:

> I will not support the Bill this evening. I have fundamental disagreements with parts of it. It requires the Government, and particularly their successors, to embark on a drastic restructuring of the British economy. There is an air of unreality about a great deal of what I have heard this evening. I doubt whether most of it will happen (Hansard 2008a: c.98).

A short while later, in the same debate, Tyrie cited criticism of the *Stern Review* by politicians and environmental economists at a symposium held at Yale University in America:

> Professor Nordhaus, probably the world's leading environmentalist, described the conclusions as "completely absurd" . . . Professor Tol said: "If a student of mine were to hand in this report as a Masters thesis, perhaps, if I were in a good mood, I would give him a 'D' for diligence; but more likely, I would give him an 'F' for fail."(Hansard 2008a: c.99).

Sammy Wilson

In June 2008 Sammy Wilson, a Democratic Unionist Party (DUP) member, became Northern Ireland's Environment Minister and, right from the start, was not afraid to make it clear he was "sceptical that all climate change is caused by CO_2 emissions" (BBC News 2008a).

Within months, not surprisingly perhaps, he was in trouble with green campaigners for describing their view on climate change as a "hysterical pseudo-religion"; adding that he believed it occurred naturally and was not man-made. However, he also said he believed that resources "should be used to adapt to the consequences of climate change, rather than King Canute-style vainly trying to stop it" (BBC News 2008b).

On New Year's Eve that year, despite ongoing criticism, he was still adamant that:

> Spending billions on trying to reduce carbon emissions is one giant con that is depriving third world countries of vital funds to tackle famine, HIV and other diseases . . . I'll not be stopped saying what I believe needs to be said about climate change . . . Most of the people who shout about climate change have not

> read one article about it. I think in 20 years' time we will look back at this whole climate change debate and ask ourselves how on earth were we ever conned into spending the billions of pounds which are going into this without any kind of rigorous examination of the background, the science, the implications of it all (*Belfast Telegraph* 31 December 2008).

As evidence of how the Internet enables comments by public figures in local government to be seized upon as legitimising propaganda by those with vested interests anywhere in the world, within a week, this interview was reproduced in full on an American website (*West Virginia Coal Association*, 5 January 2009).

This is particularly worth noting because, within weeks, Wilson was facing a vote of no confidence in the Northern Ireland assembly (although the DUP leadership declared their continuing support for him) and, although clearly mistaken, the IPCC's Professor Martin Parry said (as reported in the *Guardian* newspaper), "I do not mean to be dismissive, but I do not think—outside Northern Ireland—that anyone has heard of him . . ." (McDonald and Jowit 2009).

By 2011, Wilson had been moved to the Ministry of Finance and Personnel, but was still being very forthright about his sceptical views. In a New Year's message to readers of his blog, he began by saying:

> Nature defied all the extravagant claims of the global warming fanatics yet again, giving us weeks of below freezing temperatures and the heaviest snowfalls for fifty years, despite the claims by the so called scientific experts at the start of the decade that snowfalls in Britain would be a thing of the past because of global warming. N.I. and indeed most of Europe and N. America have struggled through the coldest winter for decades and this has not been a one-off occurrence

but part of a trend in a decade which has seen no increase in world temperatures despite rising levels of CO_2 a phenomena which has caused the Global warming fanatics to hide, change and make up data to back their increasing threadbare theories of world climate (Wilson 2011a).

In April 2011, Wilson said that this ". . . is another consequence of the madcap policies of the climate change lobby who argued for this tax in order to save the world from 'rising temperatures'" (Wilson 2011b).

One could be forgiven for thinking that Wilson just likes being controversial but, if so, surely he would have re-considered his choice of words since being removed from his post as Environment Minister. On the contrary, however, his website retains a very full and frank summary of his views on the subject:

> Our climate is changing; there is little doubt that global warming had taken place in the last 30 years of the 20th century. However actual evidence (not forecasted computer models) now shows us that the earth has actually been cooling since 1998. I dispute the theory, and it is only a theory, that the world is warming due to CO_2 emissions and other human activity. Throughout the history of the earth temperatures have fluctuated, and we know this due to records which state that grapes used to be able to be grown in Scotland during Roman times and ice skaters could be seen on the Thames during the Victorian era. We have witnessed a period of global warming towards the end of the 20th century and we are now entering into a cooler period. These have occurred due to the natural variations in the temperature of the planet, not because of human activity (Wilson 2011c).

Sammy Wilson's autobiographical entry on his website makes it clear that he has an economics background; having been educated ". . . at Methodist College Belfast, he went on to graduate in Economics and Politics from Queens University Belfast" (Wilson 2011d). After completing postgraduate teaching training, Wilson took up a teaching post at Grosvenor Grammar School and, after a very successful career in teaching (becoming Head of Economics and Assistant Chief Examiner for A-Level Economics in Northern Ireland), he first entered public office, as a Belfast City Councillor, in 1981 (ibid).

Others

Sonja Boehmer-Christiansen

Dr Sonja Boehmer-Christiansen (SBC) is an Emeritus Reader within the Dept. of Geography at the University of Hull and, since 1998, has been the Editor of the *Energy and Environment* (E&E) Journal.[m] However, as she admits herself, she has a long track-record of eschewing conventional thinking: "I was born . . . with much natural curiosity and the desire to argue rather than believe" (Spiked—undated online interview).

In 2002, she co-authored an assessment of the reasons for the failure of the Kyoto (UNFCCC) Process,[n] which is very revealing: For example, a chapter entitled 'The suppression of scientific controversy' begins by asserting that ". . . climate change science has been selectively interpreted by the IPCC . . ."; and that ". . . IPCC spokesmen acceded to what we consider to be unwarranted alarmism on the part of [non-state] actors" (SBC and Kellow 2002: 148). Furthermore, whist admitting their inability to deal with the science in detail, the authors claimed they were confident they could show ". . . how the IPCC has tended towards generating a particular kind of consensus: one that would serve to bias policy towards emission reduction and hence attacks on coal and oil in particular"° (ibid: 149). Finally, despite the fact that the IPCC is widely acknowledged to be overly-conservative in its reports (e.g. in Biello 2007), the authors claim that the IPCC ". . . systematically constructs the available science so as to downplay uncertainty, accentuate human causality, magnify the likely warming and depict it as harmful in its consequences" (ibid: 161).

Not only is this a complete inversion of reality but, an objective reader could be forgiven for concluding that the whole book is an attempt to generate controversy for its own sake. However, this is consistent with SBC's autobiographical *raison d'être* (see *Spiked* interview above), as well as that of the E&E journal that she edits, the Mission Statement of which includes the acknowledgement that it has:

> . . . consistently striven to publish many 'voices' and to challenge conventional wisdoms. Perhaps more so than other European energy journal, the editor has made E&E a forum for more sceptical analyses of 'climate change' and the advocated solution (E&E Journal *Mission Statement*).

However, the E&E journal has been repeatedly criticised for accepting papers for publication that no major peer-reviewed scientific journal would accept (Thacker 2005); culminating in the criticism of the Independent Review of the UEA/CRU email scandal by Sir Muir Russell, wherein Boehmer-Christiansen is quoted has having told the Inquiry:

> As editor of a journal which remained open to scientists who challenged the orthodoxy, I became the target of a number of CRU manoeuvres. The hacked emails revealed attempts to manipulate peer review to E&E's disadvantage, and showed that libel threats were considered against its editorial team [and the] desire to control the peer review process in their favour is expressed several times (Russell 2010: 66).

However, in addition to generally finding no evidence of scientific fraud on the part of the CRU, the Inquiry specifically concluded that:

> . . . [there is] nothing in these exchanges or in Boehmer-Christiansen's evidence that supports any allegation that CRU has directly and improperly attempted to influence the journal that she edits. Jones' response to her accusation of scientific fraud was appropriate, measured and restrained (ibid).

Philip Foster

In the 2nd edition of *While the Earth Endures*, Foster repeatedly refers to the cause of ACD as the "greenhouse hypothesis"; and therefore disputes the fact that ACD could be happening at all because: (1) a greenhouse becomes warm by preventing convection rather than trapping reflected radiation (as per Prof R.W. Wood's experiment of 1909) and (2) the transfer of heat from a cooler atmosphere to a warmer surface would violate the second law of thermodynamics (2010: 223-7).[p] Foster also favours the view that CO_2 is not a pollutant; and that apparent warming is mainly due to the systematic error of the "heat island" effect (ibid: 127-30). He also cites eight "baseless fears" of environmentalism in general and climate science in particular (ibid: 131-9);[q] criticises climate models [which he says can probably be dismissed as "being irrelevant"] (ibid: 156-63); and dismisses the MBH98 "hockey stick" graph as a scientific fraud (ibid 166-7).

However, on the occasion of *Climate Fools Day*, Foster was quoted by Louise Gray in the *Daily Telegraph* newspaper, as having said that:

> [The Climate Change Act 2008] will cost taxpayers £480bn over the next 40 years because of the cost of new technologies like wind farms . . . There is no

evidence that human input has anything to do with global temperatures . . . Therefore we should not be wasting any money on climate change through things like this legislation (quoted in Gray 2010).

Therefore, leaving aside his reliance upon the supposed economic arguments for not taking any action to mitigate ACD, his undoubtedly earnestly-held view that ACD is not happening has required him, first and foremost, to reject any and all evidence that it is.

Lord Monckton

Despite the nature of his Tertiary education, the De-Smog Blog notes that Monckton is cited as a "Global Warming expert" by the Heartland Institute; and as the "Chief Policy Advisor" of the Science and Public Policy Institute (SPPI).

The latter is a US-based organisation (as is the Heartland Institute) and thus is not analysed separately. However, given that the SPPI's website declares its Mission is to provide ". . . research and educational materials dedicated to sound public policy based on sound science . . . [and to] support the advancement of sensible public policies rooted in rational science and economics" (SPPI 2010), it is difficult to see how Monckton's Classics background qualifies him for the position of SPPI's Chief Policy Advisor. Nevertheless, Monckton continues to be able to publish several articles without going through any peer-review process.[r]

In typically-bold fashion, Monckton has published (via SPPI) a critique of a speech made by (US Presidential Science Advisor) John Holdren on 6 September 2010 entitled, *Climate-Change Science and Policy: What Do We Know? What Should We Do?* This critique, entitled *"Unsound Advice"*, provides a good summary of Monckton's position, which is that ACD stopped in 2001, current warmth is not unprecedented, some glaciers are advancing, and sea levels are not rising, *etc.* (Monckton 2010: 2-6).[s]

Monckton continues: "Dr. Holdren then turns to the causes of 'global warming' [and] parrots the IPCC in attributing nearly all of the warming since 1750 to Man's emissions of greenhouse gases" (ibid: 7). Therefore, at best, Monckton appears to question the IPPC's independence and, at worst, he appears to ridicule its conclusions. However, he then goes on to criticise Holdren's reliance on the output of climate models:

> Dr. Holdren uses one of the oldest dodges in the armoury of pseudo-science: he says that if he compares human and natural influences on the climate from 1880 to 2005 he finds that what he calls a "state-of-the-art" climate model will faithfully "predict" the ups and downs of climate over the period. This is simply voodoo. There are so many tunable parameters in every climate model that it is always possible to make a few tweaks and thus force the model to reproduce past climate changes (ibid: 8).

Not only is the language and form of argument unscientific, it is, arguably, a deliberate ploy to mimic criticism more-often made of climate change sceptics themselves.

Monckton then moves on to ridicule dire warnings about the potential impacts of ACD (ibid: 9-10).[t] Similarly, Holdren's focus on the recent extreme weather conditions in various places around the globe are dismissed as local phenomena and evidence of natural variability (ibid 10-11).[u]

Finally, Monckton concludes with another bold—but completely unsubstantiated—statement that:

> "Any measures to cut CO_2 emissions that are affordable will make no difference to the climate. Any

cuts in CO_2 emissions that might in theory make some difference to the climate are unaffordable" (ibid: 14).

Thus, it may be seen that, not satisfied with ridiculing the work of thousands of scientists in hundreds of countries, Monckton's trump card is an economic one; and he clearly believes that the consensus view is mistaken. Moreover, even if warming may happen and may be significant (and it is a big "if" in his mind), he does not accept that radical change in human behaviour is required. Thus he may best be characterised as a Promethean and, at worst, an outright Contrarian.

Benny Peiser

According to the De-Smog Blog, Benny Peiser has published 3 research papers in peer-reviewed journals; none of which is related to human-induced climate change. Furthermore it cites Peiser himself, in an article for the *Times Higher Education* supplement on 4 September 2008, as freely admitting that ". . . I'm not a climate scientist and have never claimed to be one . . . My interest is in how climate change is portrayed as a potential disaster and how we respond to that" (De-Smog Blog—Benny Peiser).

As such, however, Peiser has become notorious for criticising Dr Naomi Oreskes for a study, published in *Science* in 2004.[v] As De-Smog Blog records:

> Peiser's "claim to fame" in the war on climate change science was a 2005 study that he claimed refuted an earlier study by [Oreskes] . . . Peiser originally stated . . . that Oreskes was incorrect and that "in light of the data [he] presented . . . *Science* should withdraw Oreskes' study and its results in order to prevent any further damage to the integrity of science" (ibid).

As recorded by the Skeptical Science website (subtitled 'Getting sceptical about global warming scepticism'):

> Benny Peiser repeated Oreskes survey and claimed to have found 34 peer reviewed studies rejecting the consensus. However, an inspection of each of the 34 studies reveals most of them don't reject the consensus at all. The remaining articles in Peiser's list are editorials or letters, not peer-reviewed studies. [Therefore] Peiser has since retracted his criticism of Oreskes survey: "Only [a] few abstracts explicitly reject or doubt the ACD . . . consensus which is why I have publicly withdrawn this point of my critique . . . I do not think anyone is questioning that we are in a period of global warming. Neither do I doubt that the overwhelming majority of climatologists is agreed that the current warming period is mostly due to human impact" (Peiser as quoted by *Skeptical Science*).

Notwithstanding the retraction of his claims, Peiser went on to team up with Lord Lawson to co-found the GWPF in 2009 and, although he now leaves others to attack the science, he is still not above repeating the message (albeit subliminal and wrapped up in an psychological context) that ACD is not a problem worth worrying about:

> The global warming hysteria is well and truly over. How do we know? Because all the relevant indicators—polls, news coverage, government u-turns and a manifest lack of interest among policy makers—show a steep and deepening decline in public concern about climate change . . . Public opinion is the crucial factor that determines whether policy makers advance or abandon contentious policies . . . Media coverage of climate change has dropped sharply . . . The public's concern about global warming as a pressing problem is in marked decline not least because of the growing realisation

that governments and the international community are ignoring the advice of climate campaigners . . . [Governments] are assisted in this policy of benign neglect by a public that has largely become habituated to false alarms and is happy to ignore other claims of environmental catastrophe that are today widely disregarded or seen as scare tactics (Peiser 2011).

Sadly, all of what Peiser says here may be true but, is this unfair criticism of his motives? He is a social anthropologist after all. However, whatever his area of expertise, if he wanted to point out that people should be concerned about ACD, he could have surely found some way to do so (as indeed Hamilton has done)? His apparent contentment with a policy of "benign neglect" is therefore either Prometheanism or Economic Rationalism. Given his association with Lawson, the latter would seem to be a more appropriate categorisation.

Bruno Prior

Bruno Prior is the Director of Summerleaze Ltd who, when invited to contribute a 'Foreword' for Robinson's IEA publication in 2008, started by listing all the things that scientists who fear ACD claim they know[w] and therefore demand that something must be done. However, Bruno describes this "something" as an asymmetric precautionary principle:

> . . . which demands precaution against the risk that today's freedoms may harm future generations more than they benefit present generations, but opposes precaution against the risk that today's constraints may harm present generations more than they benefit future generations (Prior 2008: 12).

Quoting Bertrand Russell as having said 'the whole problem with the world is that fools and fanatics are always so certain of themselves, but wiser people so full of doubts' Bruno concludes that:

> We do not need to nationalise or regulate to have a centrally planned economy. We can do it just as effectively with incentives. The successful 'entrepreneur' is no longer someone who innovates to provide . . . the goods that people want, but someone who has persuaded government to back his version of the future (ibid: 14).

Stephen Wilde

Whereas his detractors point out that he is not listed as a Fellow of the RMS on their website, Wilde himself has repeatedly pointed out that this is because he became a Fellow before scientific qualifications became a mandatory prerequisite. For example, see the Pete's Place blog (and comments) [online].[x] Whilst there is no evidence of intentional fraud, the fact remains that he is not a scientist and—as such—does not appear to have ever had anything published in a peer-reviewed scientific journal (RMS or otherwise).

However, given that two of Wilde's posts are in the all-time top three most-read articles on the CR website, they seem to demand attention. The following is typical:

> It is true that, as the alarmists say, since 1961 the average level of TSI [total solar irradiance] has been approximately level . . . those solar cycles show substantially higher levels of TSI than have ever previously occurred in the historical record. Because of the height of the TSI level one cannot simply ignore it as the IPCC and the modellers have done. The critical issue is that . . . the sun was already producing more heat than was required to maintain a stable Earth temperature. On that basis alone the theory of ACD cannot be sustained and should now die (Wilde 2008).

Not only is the language used unscientific and prejudicial, it is an assertion of unsubstantiated opinion masquerading as one of scientific fact. It is no more valid than to point out that anthropogenic emissions of CO_2 represent less than 1% of what is in the atmosphere without acknowledging that these additional emissions (of fossilised carbon) are upsetting the dynamic equilibrium of the rock cycle that has remained fairly constant over recent geological time (i.e. since the formation of the Himalayas 55 million years ago).

Most recently (30 May 2011), Wilde has yet again criticised the peer-reviewed work of established climate scientists using unprofessional language:

> They did not realise that although the regional changes were most apparent those changes did in fact reflect a change in the global energy budget from net warming to net cooling or vice versa . . . They were probably thrown by the observation of a cooling stratosphere whilst the sun was more active when the established ideas would have expected a warming stratosphere from a more active sun . . . Although they explicitly acknowledge the modulating bottom up effect of oceanic oscillations they do not follow through . . . They even acknowledge that energy input to the oceans is affected but fail to link it explicitly to cloudiness and global albedo changes . . . Their consideration of ozone effects does not consider the mesosphere and it is there that I think the main error arises for established climatology. It is the solar effect on the mesosphere that drives the reverse sign solar temperature effect for both mesosphere and stratosphere as I have explained elsewhere (Wilde 2011).

However, is it not reasonable to ask why, if he is so sure of his (absent) facts, he does not get his work published in peer-reviewed journals himself? The conclusion that is almost impossible to escape is that he does not do so because no such journal would publish such opinion-based material.[y]

---

[a] Founded by one of the most prominent American sceptics (Oreskes and Conway), the late Fred Singer.
[b] A mode of argumentation that seeks to establish a contention by deriving an absurdity from its denial, thus arguing that a thesis must be accepted because its rejection would be untenable (International Encyclopaedia of Philosophy <http://www.iep.utm.edu/reductio/>)
[c] In this context, he even quoted the CRU's Phil Jones as having said, "conclusions are dependent upon the quality of the basic data" (Strangeways 2008).
[d] In support of this claim, Lawson cited the 2005-06 report of a House of Lords Select Committee (of which he was a member), which must, in light of accumulating evidence of accelerating change (e.g. summer melting of Arctic sea ice), already be considered woefully out-of-date.
[e] This is, of course, the first of Henson's possible positions that sceptics adopt (Henson 2008: 257).
[f] This conveniently ignores the fact that the current annualised release of 3 million years-worth of fossilised carbon into the atmosphere represents a significant destabilising effect upon the dynamic equilibrium of the atmosphere over recent geological time.
[g] Whilst Lawson is happy to accuse these "alarmists" of "cherry-picking" data, he is very careful to hide the one-sided nature of the (IEA) sceptical "cherry-picked" analysis of the science (by non-scientists) on which he generally relies. Given his opening remarks regarding the nature of the "debate", this is deeply ironic.
[h] Including the Rev. Thomas Mathus' *Principle of Population* (1798), Rachel Carson's *Silent Spring* (1962), Paul Ehrlich's *The Population Bomb* (1968), The Club of Rome's *Limits to Growth* (1972), and Lowell Ponte's *The Cooling* (1976).

THE DENIAL OF SCIENCE

i   Watermelons feature frequently on Delingpole's blog; e.g. item posted on 19 November 2010. Available at <http://blogs.telegraph.co.uk/news/jamesdelingpole/100064423/on-the-anniversary-of-climategate-the-watermelons-show-their-true-colours/> [accessed 10/06/2011].

j   From historical proxy (pre-instrumental) data alone, there remains evidence for the MWP (1000-1400AD) having been slightly warmer-than average; and for the Little Ice Age (1400-1900AD) having been slightly colder-than-average.

k   See the 'Archive' page of his own website, with links to articles he has written and had published on various websites around the globe: <http://brendanoneill.co.uk/private/416164141/tumblr_kyiu79fd3B1qzl21l> [accessed 14/06/2011].

l   Available at <http://www.spiked-online.com/index.php?/site/article/2948/> [accessed 13/06/2011].

m   Described by Michael Ashley (Professor of Astronomy at the University of NSW) as "the climate sceptic's journal of choice" (in a review of Ian Plimer's book "*Heaven and Earth*") in *The Australian* newspaper of 9 May 2009 [online]. Available at <http://www.theaustralian.com.au/news/ian-plimer-heaven-and-earth/story-e6frg8no-1225710387147> [accessed 17/07/2011].

n   i.e. *International Environmental Policy: Interests and the Failure of the Kyoto Process.*

o   However, they do not explain what the IPCC would gain from such an attack being made.

p   However, this over-simplistic analysis does not acknowledge that (1) the greenhouse analogy is imperfect and (2) the blanket effect of CO_2 in the atmosphere does not trap all reflected radiation (it is scattered in all directions) and, although it does indeed not warm the ground, some of it does warm the atmosphere.

q   Namely that we face (1) dramatic sea level rise; (2) more frequent extreme weather; (3) shortages of water; (4) increased prevalence of disease; (5); disruption to oceanic circulation currents (6) widespread species extinctions; (7) mass starvation; and (8) long-term elevated atmospheric CO_2 concentrations.

r   Although this does not seem to deter people from citing him as an "expert"; he has even appeared before Congressional Hearings in the USA. However, given his background, his information is always s   second-hand and, presumably, supplied by the Heartland Institute *et al*.

s   For each and every statement, Monckton quotes from—but does not properly reference—(an extreme minority of) contrarian studies.

t   This included suggesting both that areas of permafrost are not melting and/or that such melting may be beneficial; and dismissing consequential methane release as a local problem related to poor maintenance of a Russian gas pipeline.

u   It is unclear whether Monckton inadvertently or deliberately misses Holdren's point about such things happening with increasing frequency and severity.

v   This had surveyed nearly 1000 peer-reviewed abstracts and not found a single one dissenting from the consensus view that climate change is being primarily caused by human activity.

w   A classic basis for presenting a "straw man" argument.

x   Available at <http://petesplace-peter.blogspot.com/2008/05/myth-of-man-caused-global-warming.html> [accessed 31/05/2011].

y   To use a military analogy, this is the asymmetric (guerrilla) warfare used by terrorists. Furthermore, unlike the most sceptical scientists who question the motivation of those that adhere to the consensus view, Wilde appears to question their intelligence. This may explain his outstanding popularity in cyberspace; because no specialist knowledge is required to understand the points being made. However, is it really plausible that a non-scientist could have spotted errors in the work of the hundreds of scientists that have had an input into the reports produced by the IPCC? Probably not.

Printed in Great Britain
by Amazon.co.uk, Ltd.,
Marston Gate.